Anne & Emmett

Also by Thomas Fensch . . .

Steinbeck and Covici:
    The Story of a Friendship

Conversations with John Steinbeck

The FBI files on Steinbeck

Essential Elements of Steinbeck

Steinbeck's bitter fruit:
    from The The Grapes of Wrath to Occupy Wall Street

The Man Who Was Dr. Seuss;
    The Life and Work of Theodor Geisel

Of Sneetches and Whos and the Good Dr. Seuss:
    Essays on the Life and Work of Theodor Geisel

The Man Who Was Walter Mitty:
    The Life and Work of James Thurber

Conversations with James Thurber

The Man Who Changed His Skin:
    The Life and Work of John Howard Griffin

Behind Islands in the Stream: Hemingway, Cuba, the FBI
    and the crook factory

Oskar Schindler and His List:
    The Man, the Book, the Film, the Holocaust and Its
    Survivors Foreshadowing Trump:

Trump characters, Ethics, Morality and Fascism in
    Classic Literature

Timeless (Pen) Names:
    The Life and Work of Charles Lutwidge Dodgson,
    Samuel Langhorne Clemens, Eric Blair and Theodor Geisel

The Kennedy–Khrushchev Letters

Orwell in America

The Books That Haunt Us

Masters of Despair

. . . and others . . .

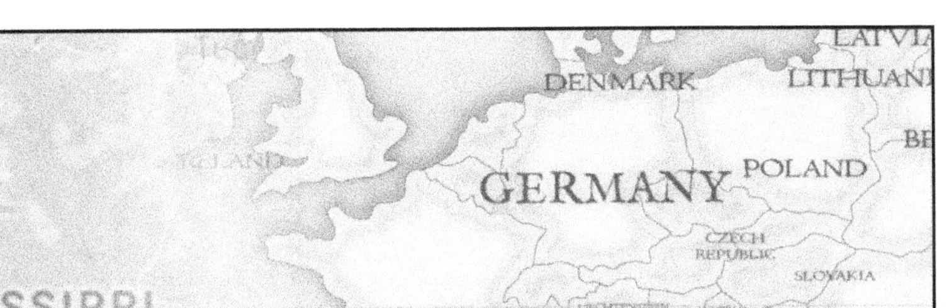

Anne & Emmett

The tragic deaths and enduring legacies of
Anne Frank and **Emmett Till**

Thomas Fensch

New Century Books
Publishing trade books and ebooks since January, 2000.
8821 Rockdale Rd.
N. Chesterfield, Va. 23236
newcentbks@gmail.com

ISBN 979-8-9856839-5-0 (hardcover)
ISBN 979-8-9856839-6-7 (paperback)
ISBN 979-8-9856839-7-4 (ebook)

The author gratefully acknowledges
Ms. Polly Arnold's exceptional proofreading.

Book design by Jill Ronsley, suneditwrite.com

for my father

Edwin A. Fensch, Ph.D.

And a little child shall lead them …
—Isaiah 11:5

The past is never dead. It's not even past.
—William Faulkner

Contents

Introduction

Uglybeautiful Stories ...

These are uglybeautiful stories.
The words and thoughts cannot be separated.
The sentiments.
They are both uglybeautiful stories.
Initial tragedy, followed by triumph of the human spirit.

Anne Frank

The Frank family, father, mother, older sister Margot and younger sister Anne, were living in Amsterdam when the Nazis invaded. They hid in their "Secret Annex," eventually joined by four others.

For over two years they remained in hiding, in cramped rooms, never going outside. Never even appearing at windows for fear that an outsider might see faces in the windows where there shouldn't be any faces.

During those weeks and months Anne kept a diary which she never allowed others to read. Written when she was 13, 14 and 15. Her teenage hopes and dreams, descriptions of the others, episodes, anecdotes. Week after week, month by month, she kept writing her diary entries.

Eventually, an acquaintance betrayed them and they were caught by the Nazis. Of the eight in the Secret Annex, only one returned to Amsterdam after the war. All the others perished.

Anne and Margot eventually were sent to Bergen-Belsen, a Nazi death camp. Both died there. Anne was 15. The Second World War ended six weeks later. They almost made it.

Her diary was found in the debris of the Secret Annex. Her father—who survived—read it and was astonished at Anne's entries, her sophistication, her writing, her thoughts and dreams.

The diary was first published after the war, with little expectation of much success; it was, after all, only the diary of a teenaged girl.

It was published under the title *The Diary of a Young Girl.* Over the years, it has sold thirty million copies world-wide.

30,000,000 copies.

Students, teenagers, anywhere in the world, could read it and say, "She's just like me."

Counting pass-along copies in libraries, the readership is surely more than that.

Anne's diary became one of the most consequential books of the twentieth century.

Emmett Till

Emmett Till was born in Chicago and lived in a suburb of Chicago.

At 14, he wanted to travel to Mississippi to visit distant relatives. His mother Mamie, was born in Mississippi and knew all too well the hazards of a Black—any Black—person in Mississippi during those years.

She warned him that life was different in Mississippi, a state sweltering in undisguised race hatred.

He took the train to visit his uncle Moses Wright.

Once there he and others his age went to a country store in Money, Mississippi, where the "encounter" took place. Others went in and out, then Emmett went in. He and a white woman, Carolyn Bryant, who with her husband owned the store, were the only two in the store at the time.

He bought bubblegum.

Did he is ask her for a date? Did he grab her arm and say "don't worry I've been with white women before"? Exactly what happened will never be known.

What were her emotions? Was she fearful, anxious, furious—was she running solely on adrenaline momentarily?

She did run outside to a car and grab a gun. She said later that she thought she would be raped.

Outside others heard a whistle. Did Emmett Till whistle at her? A leering "wolf whistle"—a sexual come-on? That alone, from a Black man of any age to a white woman, was a death sentence in Mississippi at the time.

The other Black teenagers fled in fear. Emmett Till left with them.

Carolyn Byrant told her husband, Roy Bryant. He told his half-brother J.W. "Big" Milam. Roy Byrant and Big Milam vowed to find *that nigger boy*. They went to Moses Wright's sharecropper's house and kidnapped Till in the dark of a Mississippi night.

They beat him horrifically and shot him the head. They anchored his body with a fan from a cotton gin, and threw his body into the Tallahatchie River, assuming no one would ever find it. But it surfaced several days later—surfaced just enough for others to discover the body. White officials there—notably the Sheriff—wanted to bury the body quickly and thus bury the story, but Mamie Till refused to let her son be buried in

Mississippi. She had his body returned to the Chicago area, where she had an open-casket funeral, to show the world what happened to her beloved son.

Thousands saw the body horrifically mutilated and grotesque from the river water. Others saw photographs in newspapers and magazines.

The emotions there were anguish and outrage.

The senseless lynching of Emmett Till, 14 at the time, and the outrage at his remains in the open casket, essentially began the Civil Rights movement in the United States, which continues to this day.

Carolyn Bryant changed her story of the encounter so much over the years she eventually never knew what the truth was.

Roy Bryant and Big Milam were tried for murder and found Not Guilty. Freed from being tried again, freed by Double Jeopardy, they then announced to the world that they had, in fact, killed Emmett Till. It was too much, far too much, even in Mississippi. They became *pariahs,* outcasts, for the rest of their lives.

There are now two federal laws named for Emmett Till, most notably the Emmett Till AntiLynching Act signed into law in 2022.

Anne Frank

Four Steps in Nazi Germany That Changed the World

February 27, 1933 - The Reichstag Fire

The Reichstag, the German Parliament building, in Berlin, was set afire on that date. The fire consumed the building—it was only completely rebuilt years later.

The fire was arson, apparently caused by Marinus van der Lubbe, a Dutch "council communist," who was arrested. In retrospect, some believe it was started by the Nazis themselves, as a "false flag" effort to blame the Communists, their sworn enemies.

Hitler had been sworn in as Chancellor only the previous January 20, 1933. After the fire, all Communist members of the Reichstag were arrested; their absence gave Hitler's Nazi party a majority in the Reichstag, making it easier to enact their objectives.

German President Paul von Hindenburg, ancient at that time, issued The Reichstag Fire decree (at Hitler's request). It specified that most civil liberties were abolished, including:

- Habeas corpus;
- Freedom of expression;

- Freedom of the press;
- The right of free association;
- The right to secrecy in the mails and on telephones.

These were not reinstated during the Nazi regime.

The Nazis began a ruthless confrontation with their communist arch-enemies. Before the fire, Nazi propaganda claimed that the only way to stop the communists was to put the Nazi party in complete control of the Reichstag.

Mass arrests of thousands of communists were conducted after the fire by Nazi-controlled police.

Marinus van der Lubbe went on trial for arson and attempting to overthrow the (German) government. He was found guilty and killed by guillotine in Saxony, January 10, 1934.

Walter Gempp was then head of the Berlin Fire Department and was subsequently dismissed when he presented evidence that the Nazis were actually behind the fire. He was arrested and sent to prison. He was strangled and killed there on May 2, 1939.

The Reichstag Fire and the subsequent changes in German law marked a crucial point in the change from a democratic Germany to a Nazi-controlled dictatorship.

1933-1945—The Death Camps

*"A thousand years will pass
and the guilt of Germany will not be erased."*

Who said that?

A thousand years …

Anne Frank?
Her father Otto Frank?
Someone else in hiding with the Franks?

It was Hans Frank, head of the Nazi government in Poland when Poland was occupied.

Hans Frank (no relation to the Otto Frank family) was an early member of the German Workers' Party, precursor of the Nazi party. He took part in the infamous Beer Hall Putsch, November 8-9, 1923, which failed. He became principal lawyer for the Nazi party. In June 1934, he was named *Reichleiter* (Reich Leader). In December, 1934, he joined the Hitler cabinet.

When Nazi Germany invaded Poland in 1939, he was appointed Governor-General of occupied Poland. He began a reign of terror and was directly involved in the mass murder of Jews and others. He used forced labor and was principal supervisor of four extermination camps. He remained head of the Nazi government of Poland until it collapsed in 1945.

Over four million people were murdered under his jurisdiction.

After the war he was brought before the Nuremberg war crimes courts.

He might have thought that his *thousand years* comment might save him; he was found guilty of war crimes and was executed by hanging October, 1946.

More than anything else, the death camps and the deaths of millions of Jews—adults *and* children like Anne Frank—and other ethnic and national groups—is the defining—and damning—legacy of Hitler's Germany.

Germany's loss in World War I sparked the anti-semitism that would become the Holocaust.

It began with a lie: it was the fault of the Jews.

In his massive study, *The Holocaust*, Martin Gilbert writes:

But in the turmoil of defeat, voices were blaming 'the Jews' for Germany's humiliation, In Berlin, the nation's capital, there were clashes between Jews and anti-semites. 'Indications of growing anti-semitism, the Berlin correspondent for *The Times* reported, on August 14, 1919, 'are becoming frequent."

A manifestation of this anti-semitism was shown by one of Germany's newest and tiny political parties, the National Socialist German Workers' Party, the NSDAP, soon better known as the 'Nazi' Party, after the first two syllables of "National'—*Nazional.* The party's twenty-five point programme was published in Munich on 25 February 1920, at a time when it had only sixty members. The essence of the programme was nationalistic, the creation of a 'Great Germany', and the return of Germany's colonies, which had been lost at the time of Germany's defeat. Point four was a racialist one; 'None but members of the Nation,' it read, 'may be citizens of the State. None but those of German blood, whatever their creed, may be members of the Nation. No Jew, therefore, may be a member of the Nation.' Another point demanded that all Jews who had come to Germany since 1914 should be forced to leave: a demand which would affect more than eighteen thousand Jews, most of them born in the Polish provinces of Tsarist Russia.

The anti-Jewish section of the Nazi Party's program had been drafted by three members. One of them, Adolf Hitler, was member seven in the party's hierarchy. A former soldier on the western front, he had been wounded and gassed in October 1918, less than a month before the war's end. On 13 August 1920, Hitler spoke for two hours in a Munich beer cellar on the theme, 'Why we are against the Jews.' During his speech he promised his listeners that his party, and his party alone, 'will free you from the power of the Jew.' There must, he said, be a new slogan and one not only for Germany—"Anti-Semites of the World, Unite! People of Europe, Free Yourselves!' And he demanded what he called a 'through solution', in brief, 'the removal of the Jews from the midst of our people'.

Where did Hitler's anti-semitism come from?
In large part, from America.

While he was building his automobile empire and the assembly lines and the promised five dollars a day for his workers (who could then afford to buy his Model T Fords), Henry Ford bought a local weekly newspaper *The Dearborn* (Michigan) *Independent,* solely as a vehicle for his anti-semitism. He railed against the Jews in column after column; "The International Jew—The World's Problem" appeared on the front page week after week. 80 columns in total, which became four books, *The International Jew,* vols. 1, 2, 3 and 4.

Volume One was subtitled *The International Jew*; Vol 2. *Jewish Activities in the United States*; Vol. 3, *Jewish Influence in the United States* and Vol. 4, *Aspects of Jewish Power in the United States*.

The Dearborn Independent was distributed in Ford dealerships throughout the country and given free to the public. At its peak, circulation was 700,000.

> *Henry Ford was the only American cited by name in Hitler's 1925 autobiography, Mein Kampf (My Struggle). Hitler had a picture of Ford in his office.*

Hitler reportedly said, Ford "is the single great man," essentially Hitler's hero.

Ford also adamantly opposed to jazz—which he thought was decadent—and wanted to make square dancing the national dance of the United States.

In July 1938, the German Counsel in Cleveland gave Henry Ford—on his 75th birthday—the Grand Cross of the German Eagle, the highest award Nazi Germany could bestow on a foreigner.

It can easily be said that while Henry Ford's assembly lines were producing Model Ts, Henry Ford was also producing Adolf Hitler's anti-semitism.

(And proving that racism and hatred have no boundaries.)

Aldous Huxley knew much of this (although he didn't know Ford was cited in Hitler's autobiography); he satirized Ford throughout his novel *Brave New World* (1932). *In God We Trust* became *In Ford We Trust*; the top of the Christian cross was cut off, becoming a T, representing Ford's Model T, thus making Ford a deity and his empire a religion.

The first wave of the Holocaust came in occupied Poland—in September, 1939, under Nazi Governor-General Hans Frank: the program was named *Aktion T4*, the elimination of *useless mouths*—German, Austrian and Polish hospital patients with mental or physical disabilities. Authorized by Hitler, *Aktion T4* was initiated by the SS—the *Schutstaffel*, a paramilitary arm of the Nazi Party, to eliminate those "unworthy of life." In German *Lebensunwertes Leben;* those the Nazis deemed to have *no right to life, but* simply mouths that needed to be fed and cared for, but who could not contribute to Hitler's Third Reich.

It was the first step.

By 1941, experiences in the *Aktion T4* program in secret killing of hospital patients lead to the direct creation of concentration camp and death camps for implementation of the next step.

The program named the Final Solution.

The Final Solution to the Jewish problem.

How soon were concentration camps and death camps established under Hitler?

Almost immediately.

Hitler came to power January 30, 1933; the first camp was named Nohra, established March 3, 1933. About 70 camps followed, in any location possible: vacant factories; prisons; country estates, and any other facility available.

On June 26, 1933, Heinrich Himmler appointed Theodor Eicke the second commandant of Dachau, which became the model for other camps. He established a set of rules and procedures, including the use of *kapos,* prisoners themselves who were essentially lowest-level camp police.

Himmler called for an all-out war against communists, socialists, Jews, Freemasons and criminals, among others. He was named Chief of the German police by Hitler June 17, 1936.

Camps that became world-famous—or really notorious—were Sachsenhausen, established in September, 1936, and Buchenwald, in July 1937.

Nazi raids in June, 1938, rounded up and imprisoned homeless people, the mentally ill and the unemployed.

Mauthausen was established in August, 1938 and Ravensbrück, the first camp for women prisoners, in May, 1939.

Hitler's architect, Albert Speer, had grand plans for enormous buildings in key German cities; Mauthausen and Flossenbürg were established near quarries, to supply Speer's construction projects.

After *Kristallnacht* (the "Night of Broken Glass") November 9-10, 1938, 26,000 Jewish men were sent into concentration camps, overwhelming the system.

In April, 1941, the SS ordered the murder of ill and exhausted prisoners; by the end of April, 1942 an estimated 20,000 had been killed, which marked the beginning of systematic murders in the camps. In April, 1941, the SS began killing Soviet prisoners; by the end of the project in mid-1942, an estimated 34,000 had been murdered.

Auschwitz became notorious as having the highest death rate. Jews sent there were invariably killed, often as soon as they arrived.

Military units, the SS *Einsatzgruppen,* followed the German armies, the *Wehrmacht,* as kill squads.

Camps exclusively for the extermination of Jews were established; Kulmhof. Belzec, Sobibor and Treblinka; these were specifically outside the camps system.

By late 1941, when the German Army failed to conquer Stalingrad, demands increased for war production; Himmler and Speer agreed to use prisoners for armaments production and damage repair. Sub-camps were set up near workplaces.

Eventually, by one estimate, by historian Nikolaus Wachsmann, there were *27 main camps and 1,100 sub-camps*; most outside Germany in German-invaded countries, such as Poland.

In addition to the vast concentration camp system, the Nazis used six camps simply as execution camps: Chemlo; Belzec; Sobibor; Treblinka; Majdanek and Auschwitz, also called Auschwitz-Birkenau.

In Majdanek and Auschwitz, inmates were also literally worked to death.

Jews represented 90 percent of extermination camp victims.

Nazi officials did differentiate between the concentration camps, *Vernichtungslager,* and death camps, *Todeslager.*

Death in German: *der Tod.*

An SS official, Johann Kremer later said, "Dante's inferno seems to me almost a comedy compared to this. They don't call Auschwitz the camp of annihilation for nothing."

Most of the Nazi killing camps were established in Poland, which had the largest Jewish population in Europe. Additionally, death camps outside Germany could be kept secret from the general German population.

Auschwitz and Majdanek had been parts of a massive labor complex; Belzec, Sobibor and Treblinka were established solely as killing centers, with inmates killed immediately on arrival. These camps were located on branch lines of the Polish railway system.

Later, during the Final Solution, Adolf Eichmann was in charge of making sure the death trains ran on time.

Heinrich Himmler witnessed a mass shooting outside Minsk in 1941; he was told the poor, innocent Nazi soldiers were so upset that the Auschwitz commander, Rudolf Höss, stated that the killers—the *Einsatzkommandos*—either went mad or killed themselves.

The answer: mass killings with poison gas, Zyklon B, which the *Einsatzkommandos* did not have to directly witness.

Inmates were deceived that gas chambers were simply shower rooms, but some weren't deceived; Nazi officials later said that some had mortal terror in their eyes and began screaming. Those were taken away and shot.

Höss said some high Nazi leaders witnessed the gassings in Auschwitz: "All were deeply impressed by what they saw ... yet some who had previously spoken most loudly about the necessity for this extermination fell silent once they had seen the 'final solution of the Jewish problem.'" He also said that "Adolf Eichmann, who was certainly tough enough, had no wish to change places with me."

Three crematoria were built at Auschwitz-Birkenau which burned bodies 24 hours a day; yet the death rate was so high bodies had to be burned in open-air pits.

Höss was convicted of war crimes and hung April 16, 1947.

Israeli historian Otto Dov Kulka spent his boyhood years as a prisoner, in Auschwitz; he survived the war and later remembered singing *Ode to Joy* only a few feet from a crematorium. He returned decades later. His memoir, published in 2013 is, in one word, *haunting*.

The title is equally haunting:

Landscapes of the Metropolis of Death.

A Metropolis of Death.

Auschwitz, a major complex, was built for one reason: death at a rate never seen in the world.

Estimates of the number of victims murdered in the six Nazi death campus: *2.7 million.*

September 15, 1935—The Nuremberg Laws

Hitler's Reich passed the Reichstag Fire decrees following the arson fire of the Reichstag on February 27, 1933. Those decrees were only the beginning.

The Reichstag convened a special meeting September 15, 1937, during the Nazi Party's annual Nuremberg Rally. The Reichstag passed two major laws:

- The Law for the Protection of German Blood and Honour and
- The Reich Citizenship Law.

The Reich Law for the Protection of German Blood and Honor forbade marriages and extra-marital intercourse between Jews and Germans and forbade employment of German females under 45 in Jewish households.

The Citizenship Laws declared only those of German or related blood could be German citizens; all others were classified as "state subjects" without any citizens rights. A formal decree of who was officially Jewish was passed November 13 and the Citizenship Law became effective on that date. That law was amended November 26, 1935 to define *Roma* or *Romani* (Gypsies) and blacks as "Enemies of the race-based state," which placed them in the same category as Jews.

For international publicity reasons, these laws did not take effect until after the 1936 Summer Olympics, held in Berlin (in which Hitler refused to shake hands with Black American track star Jesse Owens).

Prior to the Nuremberg Laws, a Law for the Restoration of the Professional Civil Service was passed April 7, 1933 which barred *non-Aryans* from being attorneys, and teaching in secondary schools and universities.

The Nuremberg Laws included:

Law for the Protection of German Blood and Honor

Article 1: Marriages between Jews and citizens of German or related blood are forbidden; marriages previously conducted are invalid, even if conducted abroad to circumvent this law.

Annulment proceedings can be initiated only by the state prosecutor.

Article 2: Extramarital relations between Jews and citizens of German or related blood are forbidden.

Article 3: Jews may not employ in their households female citizens of German or related blood who are under 45 years old.

Article 4: Jews are forbidden to fly the Reich or national flag or display Reich colours.

They are, on the other hand, permitted to display the Jewish colors. The exercise of this right is protected by the state.

Article 5:

1. Any person who violates the prohibition under Article 1 will be punished with prison with hard labour.

2. A male who violates the prohibition under Article 2 will be punished with prison or prison with hard labour.

3. Over the coming years, an additional 13 supplementary laws are promulgated that further marginalized the Jewish community in Germany. For example, Jewish families were not permitted to submit claims for subsidies for large families and were forbidden to transact business with Aryans.

The Nazi Reich also specified these heritage specifications:

Deutschblütiger	German	Belongs to the German race and nation
Deutschblütiger	German	Is ⅛ Jewish
Mischling Zeiten Grades	*Mixed race, second grade*	Is ¼ Jewish
Mischling	Mixed race,	⅜ or ½ Jewish
ersten grades	first degree	Only partially belongs to the German race and nation, approved to have Reich citizenship.
Jude	Jew, ¾ Jewish	Belongs to the Jewish race and community, not approved for Reich citizenship.
Jude	Jewish 100 percent	Belongs to the Jewish race and community, not approved to have Reich citizenship.

Other nations tied into the Third Reich, also adopted their versions or variations of the Nuremberg Laws including: Fascist Italy and Hungary in 1938; Romania, in 1940; Slovakia, Bulgaria and Croatia, in 1941.

Japan did not not pass such legislation, but was pressed by Nazi Germany to place Jews in Singapore and Indonesia into internment camps, when Japan occupied the Dutch East Indies and Singapore.

A nation-wide book burning was held May 10, 1933, which specifically included books by Jewish authors.

The Nuremberg Laws effectively and severely hurt Jewish communities. Those convicted of violating the newly enervated marriage laws were sentenced to prison and, when released, they were immediately re-arrested by the Gestapo and sent to concentration camps.

Aryan Germans stopped shopping at Jewish stores and stopped socializing with former Jewish friends.

A law, the "Dangerous Habitual Criminals Act," passed November 24, 1933, that defined "social misfits": the chronically unemployed, prostitutes, beggars, alcoholics, homeless vagrants, Blacks and Romani and forced them into concentration camps.

By 1934, Jewish businesses were denied access to German newspapers and denied government contracts.

When the Second World War began in 1939, about 250,000 of Germany's 437,000 Jews had emigrated to the United States, Palestine, Great Britain and other countries. Soon thereafter, it was impossible for Jewish emigres to find a country that would take them.

By 1941, all Jews in Germany and in Nazi-occupied countries and territories, were forced to wear, on the outside of their clothing, a six-pointed gold star, or the Star of David. The star became one of the defining symbols of the prejudice and barbarism of Nazi Germany.

Clothing from that period with the star affixed still exists, in the United States Holocaust Museum and elsewhere.

By mid-1941, wholesale extermination of the Jews of Europe had begun.

The Nuremberg Laws remained in place until Nazi Germany was defeated in 1945.

January 20, 1942—The Final Solution

"I will leap into my grave laughing because the feeling that I have five million human beings on my conscience is for me a source of extraordinary satisfaction".
—Adolf Eichmann, during World War II.

"I was only following orders."
—Adolf Eichmann, on trial in Israel.

On July 31, 1941, Herman Goring, Reichsmarshall of all Nazi armed forces, gave authorization to Reinhard Heydrich, chief of the Nazi Security Services, to submit a plan for a "total solution to the Jewish question."

Heydrich would coordinate all Nazi activity toward this end: deporting the complete population of occupied Europe to Siberia, as well as starving vast populations by diverting food to the German army, a plan devised by Herbert Backe, a senior SS official.. Estimates are that 4.2 million Soviet citizens: Russians; Belarusians and Ukrainians were starved by the Nazis during this plan.

By November 29, 1941, Heydrich had the plans in progress, for Wansee Conference but events changed the plans. The Soviet Army stalled the Nazi army outside Moscow and the United States entered the war after the attack at Pearl Harbor. Germany declared war on the United States December 11, 1941.

During this period, Hitler decided that all Jews in Europe would be exterminated immediately, not after the war.

Heydrich invited 14 Nazi officials to a conference center in the Berlin suburb of Wannsee January 20, 1942.

Attending were: Heinrich Müller, head of the Gestapo, Adolf Eichmann and a variety of others; at least six were simply basic bureaucrats. Eichmann was, perhaps, the lowest-ranking SS officer present; his ranking the equivalent of a U.S. Army lieutenant colonel.

Heydrich said that between 1933 and October 1941, 537,000 German, Austrian and Czech Jews had emigrated; there were approximately 11 million Jews left in Europe, only half under Nazi control. Heydrich said that Europe "would be combed from west to east" as part of the solution. Jewish-German veterans of World War One would be sent to the Theresienstadt concentration camp instead of being killed.

Heydrich gave Eichmann instructions: there would be no verbatim records of the conference. Eichmann had to translate the common, often casual conversations, into official Nazi bureaucratic terms.

The Wannsee Conference lasted less than two hours—decisions to exterminate the Jews had been made before this meeting. The Wannsee meeting did not involve the highest level Nazi officials; Hitler was not present, nor was Himmler or Goebbels. The conference was simply to determine priorities; the fate of victims of Nazi policies was to be left to the SS, solely.

Eichmann was the supervisor of the deportation to the death camps, of much of Hungary's Jewish population. Most were sent to Auschwitz where they were immediately exterminated.

By July, 1944, 437,000 of a total Hungarian Jewish population of 725,000 were lost. It was about this time that Eichmann made his "I will leap into my grave ..." comment.

Eichmann, in short, made sure the Nazi trains ran on time, with their human cargos, to the death campus.

When the war ended, he was caught by the U.S. Army and sent to a detention camp but he escaped and evaded detection in Germany until 1950, when, with the help of a few Catholic priests, who were sympathetic to the former Nazis, he used a *ratline* to escape to Argentina.

Mossad, the Israeli equivalent of the FBI, and Shin Bet, the Israeli Security Service eventually confirmed his location.

They were authorized by the highest Israeli authorities to capture Eichmann and bring him to Israel for trial.

A team of Mossad and Shin Bet agents flew to Buenos Aires on a El A1 airplane, the airline owned by Israel. They were able to kidnap Eichmann and take him to a safe house, where he and the team could not be found.

How to get him to the waiting El A1. aircraft?

There was a doctor with the Mossad and Shin Bet crew; he drugged Eichmann and they put him in an El A1 uniform. They half-carried and half dragged him through the airport.

"One of our pilots, drunk again," they told curious onlookers.

The ruse worked.

Eichmann was flown to Israel where he stood trial on 15 counts of war crimes, crimes against humanity and crimes against the Jewish people.

There was a minor contretemps when it was revealed that he was in Israeli hands. Argentina claimed it was a violation of internal law to kidnap anyone and take them out of the country. An international crime it was, but the contretemps was a minor one and soon forgotten. (Perhaps Argentina was glad to be rid of him, to prevent prolonged debate and acrimony.)

Critics also claimed that Israel was not a nation during the Second World War—it was established in 1948 and admitted to the United Nations in 1949—and thus could not try Eichmann, but Israel had written laws specifically for such cases as this.

Announcements that Eichmann had been captured and was in Israeli hands were world-wide headlines. He was the highest ranking Nazi officer caught after the war.

He was interrogated hour after hour after hour after hour by top Israeli police. The trial itself took months and he was shielded in a glass booth to prevent him from being attacked by Holocaust survivors, in the trial as witnesses.

He appeared in a black suit, obviously not the imposing SS officer's uniform he wore during the War. He did not deny the Holocaust and the millions of lives lost, but said, "I was only following orders," a far, far cry from the "I leap into my grave …" self-congratulating comment he made during the War.

"I was only following orders," became a meme used by countless others in a wide variety of situations since that time.

Hanna Arendt witnessed only about five weeks of the trial and largely depended on court transcripts for the rest, for her book *Eichmann in Jerusalem.* She did, however, use variations of the word *banal* to describe Eichmann.

banal: (def.) so lacking in originality as to be obvious and boring.

Her key phrase was *the banality of evil,* which described Eichmann—and countless others—as simply unthinking cogs in the Nazi war machine.

Eichmann was found guilty on all 15 charges and was executed by hanging June 1, 1962, in Ayalon Prison, Ramia, Israel. A quickly- constructed crematorium was used for his incineration; his ashes were scattered in the sea outside Israeli territorial waters. There was no gravesite which could be a shrine for Neo-Nazis.

The site of the Wannsee Conference, January 20, 1942, which set the Final Solution in motion, the villa Am Grossen Wannsee 56-58, is now a Holocaust Memorial and Museum.

As an aside: in February, 2023, the state of Virginia legislature had a bill pending that would prevent police and other Virginia agencies from using search warrants to seize data to compile databases of women's menstrual periods.

Virginia Republican Governor Glenn Youngkin blocked that bill. Youngkin, whom most inside and outside Virginia believe is a Trump clone—a Trump wannabe—apparently decided it was perfectly appropriate to compile such databases, even through search warrants.

The White House "is condemning Gov. Glenn Youngkin for- helping to block state legislation that would have prevented police from using search warrants to seize data about women's menstrual cycles on communication apps, but the governor isn't backing down," *The Richmond Times-Dispatch* reported, in an article "White House pounces on Youngkin's menstrual tracking bill," Feb 17.

"It is a bill that not only protects privacy, it protects women in the backdrop of these very serious, very draconian abortion bans," said Barbara Favola, a Democrat from Arlington, Va..

"I absolutely think there is hostility on the part of the governor and the administration to prevent women from getting access to reproductive health care," said state Senator Ghazala Hashmini, a Democrat from Chesterfield, Va.

The Guardian reported, Feb. 16, 2023, in the article "Virginia governor blocks bill banning police from seeking menstrual histories," that "the wrangle over menstrual data tracking has parallels with a controversy in Florida, in which high school athletics officials last week backed away from a 'humiliating' proposal requiring girls who wanted to play sports to answer questions about menstruation on medicals forms."

Adolf Eichmann and his SS colleagues never went so far as to consider compiling records on women's menstrual cycles—it was much easier to simply send women to the death camps.

But Nazi Germany did use an early IBM data card-sorting machine to compile lists of ethic minorities in areas of Nazi-occupied Europe. That IBM machine has been on display in the U.S. Holocaust Museum, in Washington, D.C.

It would not have been difficult for Eichmann, or others in the SS, to sent up lists of women's menstrual cycles and they—and their opponents—would have thought it only appropriate for Nazi Germany to do exactly that.

Is that really the reputation that Glenn Youngkin wants?

Or, as they say in the military, "is this the hill he wants to die on?"

Her Words

Words on a page.
In a notebook. Hand written. Not on a typewriter.
Her words.

Some critics later would claim she wasn't writing a true history of a Jewish family during those times.

That she wasn't writing a history of the Holocaust … there was too much outside her walls that she didn't know.

A few editors would later say that her writings were immature … superficial. (One American publishing company once turned down George Orwell's *Animal Farm* because "Americans don't buy books about animals," not realizing that it was was a complex allegory about the Russian Revolution.)

A few even suggested that what she wrote was a hoax—that her father was actually the writer—later—or maybe an American named Meyer Levin, whom she never knew. Or someone else. A hoax. A fake, a complete forgery.

Written when she was 13, going on 14—written when she was 14, going on 15. Written when she was 15.

She wanted to be a journalist, wanted to be a novelist. She probably knew that being a journalist was in the present, in the now, writing about people, interviewing again and again and again—"chasing a story," as journalists themselves say—but writing a novel would be deep inside her, consumed in a world of her imagination …

Her diary—presumably a prelude to later work —

Her diary. She called it Kitty, and referred to it as you, but perhaps she also knew instinctively, at 13 or 14 or 15, that the you would also be the universal reader, one person at time turning the pages of her diary. You, the reader.

There were other diaries written during those times. And memoirs, then and later, written by adults, by Holocaust survivors, written by veteran journalists. And later, massive histories, like Shirer's *The Rise and Fall of the Third Reich*.

Her diary, found in the debris of the *Het Achterhuis* (the *Back House* in Dutch or the *Secret Annex* in English) after she was taken away, was given casually, almost accidentally, to her father.

He became—for the rest of his days—the guardian of her diary: And *The Dairy of a Young Girl* relatively quickly became …

The most consequential book ever written about the Holocaust.

And Anne Frank has become known world-wide. And is still known world-wide; her diary now surpassing, in sales and in critical acclaim, books written by adults far older.

To date, over thirty million copies—30,000,000—have been sold, and it has been translated into over 70 languages around the world.

Written when she was 13, 14 and 15.

Anne Frank and Her Diary

... at 13 ... at 14 ... at 15

Although her diary is ink on paper, if we look again, we can see her clearly, like sepia snapshots in an aging photo album.

The first *Dairy of a Young Girl* was published in 1947, with modest expectations of success.

The Netherlands State Institute for War Documentation suspected it might be a forgery, a fraud. After extensive research which proved the diary was true and not a fraud, that organization published *The Dairy of Anne Frank: The Critical Edition.* (The English translation was published in 1989.) It consisted of Anne Frank's original diary entries (Variant or Variation A), her subsequent revisions (Variant or Variation B) and her father, Otto Frank's additional text, written after the war (Variant or Variation C).

Any or all variations, as appropriate, are published for each diary entry in *The Critical Edition.*

This book is a brick, a doorstop. 700 tightly-packed pages with very, very small type. As a life-long reader, I have had used bifocal glasses since 1985.1 can't read this text. It would take someone with the patience of a saint to trudge through this. The patience of a saint with a magnifying glass.

Otto Frank, the father, and Miriam Pressler, subsequently edited and published *Anne Frank: The Dairy of a Young Girl; The Definitive Edition.* The English translation was published in 1995. The diary entries appear largely to be B variations.

There are 187 diary entries in that volume (and in normal-sized type!). The entries are not numbered in any edition, but perhaps should be. The first was written on her 13th birthday June 12, 1942, in her red and white-checked autograph album.

Her last diary entry was August 1, 1944. On August 4, 1944, Nazi officer Karl Silberbauer, in full SS uniform, and several Dutch Nazi collaborators broke into the Secret Annex and arrested all eight.

The Otto Frank—Miriam Pressler volume, for all practical purposes, is the only analysis text needed for further study of Anne Frank's diary. (The end papers have examples of her handwriting.)

How do we see Anne Frank, through her diary entries?
She is ...

- Outwardly self-confident ... but sometimes full of self-doubts ...

In her diary entry for Tuesday, June 13, 1944, she writes:

Why is it, I often ask myself, that everyone still thinks I'm so pushy and such a know-it-all? Am I really so arrogant?

And in a footnote to her diary entry for Saturday July 15, 1945, she adds

"Deep down, the young are lonelier than the old." I read this in a book somewhere and it's stuck in my mind.
And as far as I can tell, it's true.

Now, decades after the first 1947 publication of her diary, teenagers can read translations—over 70 translations so far—in languages around the world—and think to themselves:

She's just like me.

- Has life-long dreams of being a writer.

In her entry for May 11, 1944 she writes:

> *My greatest wish is to be a journalist, and later on, a famous writer ... I'd like to publish a book called* The Secret Annex ... *it remains to be seen whether I'll succeed, but my diary can serve as the basis.*

She mentions this several times throughout her diary entries. It was her most fervent obligation to herself; a sacred vow for her future.

- Is extremely guarded and private about her diary.

In her diary entry for Monday September 21, 1942, she writes that Mrs. Van Daan, in the Secret Annex, wanted to read her diary.

"No."

Just the last page? she asks.

"No."

" ... since that particular page contained a rather unflattering description of her, "she writes.

- Understands the value and permanence of the printed word.

In one of her earliest dairy entries, June 20, 1942, she writes:

"Writing in a dairy is a really strange experience for someone like me. … I feel like writing, and have an even greater need to get things off my chest.
"Paper has more patience than people."

• Understands the plight of the Jews in the war.
In the diary entry for May 22, 1944, she writes:

"To our great sorrow and dismay, we've heard that many people have changed their attitude toward us Jews. We've been told that anti-Semitism has cropped up in circles where it would have been unthinkable. This fact has affected us all very, very deeply."

She raised that issue in diary entries far before that date.

• Terrified of the Nazis just outside the Secret Annex.

As often as she discusses the plight of the Jews during this period, she also discusses the fear of Hitler's rule, in entry after entry. As far as she is concerned, the two subjects cannot be discussed one without the other, as in that same May 1944 entry.

• She adores her father, but has less regard for her mother and mixed feelings about her older sister Margot.

Her diary entry for November 7, 1942 is a long analysis of her relationships with the other three, specifically including conflicts with her mother.

- Fascinated with her own budding maturity, becoming a woman; her monthly menstrual periods, beginning during those years.
- Adores everything Hollywood. Has movie star pictures on the wall closest to her bed.

What else do we see in her diary entries?
She …

- Would like to have a real teenaged-romance, but in the cramped Secret Annex, she knows such would be impossible and the closest boy, Peter Van Pels, also in the Secret Annex, she realizes, is too immature and too unsophisticated for her.
- Is obsessed with her appearance, her clothes and especially her hair.
- Is outgoing, usually needs to be the center of attention, is sometimes demanding.

Above all, she learned quickly—or understood intuitively—what many other, older writers never learn - the art of exceptional writing is the art of revision. She revised, many of the entries in her diary, always making the passages better, clearer, more sophisticated.

And here we can turn to Philip Roth, one of the most acclaimed novelists of his generation, also Jewish. (His parents were second- generation Americans; his mother came from Kyiv.) Along with other awards, he won the Pulitzer Prize for his 1997 novel *American Pastoral.* He died in 2018, at 85.

In his 1979 novel *The Ghost Writer,* his characters talk of Anne Frank and her diary:

"She was a marvelous young writer. She was something for thirteen. It's like watching an accelerated film of a fetus sprouting a face, watching her mastering things. You must read it. Suddenly she's discovering reflection, suddenly there's portraiture, character sketches, suddenly there's a long intricate eventful happening so beautifully recounted it seems to have gone through a dozen drafts. And no poisonous notion of being *interesting* or *serious*. She just *is*. "

And …

"The ardor in her, the spirit in her—always on the move, always starting things, being boring as unbearable to her as being bored—a terrific writer, really. And an enormously appealing child … ."

In Hiding: The Secret Annex

The denouement of this saga is in Amsterdam (and the final, final denouement is in the Nazi concentration camp Bergen-Belsen) but the story originates in Frankfurt.

Anne Frank was born in Frankfurt, June 12, 1929. When she was four, her family, who were Jewish, moved to Amsterdam at the end of 1933. Their intent was goto to evade Adolf Hitler and his Nazi party, which had taken control of Germany.

Her father had moved to Amsterdam in mid-1933 to establish the Dutch branch of the firm, Opekta-Werke, which made pectin used in jams. By May, 1940, her family was trapped in Amsterdam—the Germans had invaded the Netherlands. In 1941, she lost her German citizenship.

Their first apartment was at Merwedeplein 37. In December, 1933, Anne was living in a suburb of Amsterdam and joined the family there in February or possibly March, 1934.

Anne wrote her first diary entry there, in June, 1942, in a red and white checkered autograph album, on her thirteenth birthday.

The family soon moved to the address later made famous: Prinsenmgracht 263, where her father had moved his offices in December, 1940.

The Nazis issued call-up notices for all Jews, in June, 1942. The Franks had received a letter from Nazi officials informing them that one of them must appear for a transport train to Westerbork, a transit camp, to the far northeast section of the Netherlands. (And then to where? Nazi Germany? Other Nazi-dominated countries? Eventually from Westerbork ... to where?) Instructions were: take a suitcase; two blankets; food for three days; a towel; toilet articles; a plate, a cup and a spoon. Winter shoes, underwear, overalls.

At first glance, they initially assumed that Otto, the father, would be called; but the *letter specifically said Margot,* the oldest daughter.

They then knew they had to hide.

They would be hunted down if they attempted to travel and cross the borders in search of freedom elsewhere.

They hid in the *Het Achterhuis* (the *Back House* in Dutch; the *Secret Annex* in English) for two years and one month.

Where or what was it?

it was primarily the floors above the offices where Otto Frank worked. The third and fourth floors. The ground floor was warehousing and such; the second floor offices, the third and fourth floors extended toward the back, thus *The Back House.*

The third floor had a door leading back toward the *Back House,* the *Secret Annex.* A bookcase was subsequently built onto the front of the door; it could be locked from the back side, so the bookcase/door simply looked like a bookcase.

The third floor had six rooms, three on one side of a stairwell, three storerooms on the other side; apparently never designed as an apartment. It would have been adequate—but only barely adequate—for a couple, not for all those who hid there. The fourth floor had one major room, and an attic.

And who hid from the Nazis in the *Het Achterhuis*? In *The Secret Annex'*?

- Otto Frank and his wife, Edith;
- Hermann and Augusta van Pels, family friends;
- Their son Peter;
- A dentist, Fritz Pfeffer (originally Miep Geis's dentist) and
- Anne and her older sister Margot.

Eight—six adults—counting Peter van Pels as an adult, plus the two girls, in empty rooms and storage rooms never planned for an apartment, even one just for two.

And Anne, on the cusp of womanhood, expecting her monthly menstrual periods to begin any time during those years, was constantly mortified that she often had to share impossibly small rooms with an adult male—the dentist Fritz Pfeffer; all the more mortified, as she bloomed physically and sexually into a young woman. (Her parents assumed that this arrangement was appropriate, as they equally assumed that Anne was still very much a child. Anne and Margot had shared a room, but when Pfeffer arrived, Margot moved into the bedroom with her mother and father. Anne then had to share a room with Pfeffer.)

When she changed names in her diary, Pfeffer's name became Albert Dussel (trans.—Albert Dope).

And sometimes she had to argue, or at least negotiate, with Pfeffer, for the use of a tiny writing table, when she wanted to write her diary entries. Her father finally had to intervene and broker a schedule between the two of them, for the use of the tiny table.

Her diary entry for Tuesday July 13, 1943 describes in detail her feud with Dussel about the tiny table and the schedule for each to use it.

Anne and Pfeffer never did become friends, Melissa Muller writes.

What couldn't the eight do in hiding?

• *Go out freely.*

Only a few people working in the offices on the ground floor knew of the eight above them. If someone—anyone—from *The Het Achterhuis* came out during the day into the open, the secret was out. And they likely could be caught by the Nazis or their Dutch collaborators at any time.

They had no fresh air in over two years.

• *Make any sort of noise.*

Even shoes on wooden floors might be audible from below. Better to always go without shoes when there were workers below, as Miep Gies eventually explained in her memoir, *Anne Frank Remembered.* The office workers had no reason to suspect there was anyone in the upper floors, much less eight people.

• *Be careful at windows.*

Faces seen inside—from the outside—might be trouble. Faces inside where there shouldn't be faces.

• *The children couldn't go to school.*

(Anne changed the names of friends in her Diary entries; the van Pelts became the van Daans. Miep Gies used Anne's names.) As Gies writes:

> Mr. Frank was the supervisor of the children's studies
> up in the hiding place. Rigorous studying was expected;

assignments were corrected by Mr. Frank. Because Peter van Daan was not much of a student, Mr. Frank made a point of taking extra time and care with him. Otto Frank would have made a wonderful teacher; he was kind and firm, and always included a little bit of humor with his lessons.

The children's studies took great chunks of time each day. For Margot, it was easy. As for Anne, although she didn't concentrate as hard as Margot, it was easy too. Anne was often writing in a little red-orange checkered cloth-bound diary that her father had given her for her thirteenth birthday on June 12, several weeks before the Franks had gone into hiding. She wrote in her diary in two places, her own room or her parents' room. Although everyone knew that she was writing, she never wrote when there were people present. Obviously, Mr. Frank had spoken about this matter and given instructions for no one to disturb her.

As I heard from Mr. Frank, the diary was a constant companion for Anne, and also the cause of teasing by the others. How was she finding so much to write about? Anne's cheeks went pink when she was teased. She would tease right back, always quick with a reply, but to be safe, she kept her diary in her father's old leather briefcase.

How to get food and supplies into the Secret Annex? Those eight inside needed friends—to bring food and supplies, empty garbage to the outside, bring family news, Amsterdam news, news of the war and—especially to bring emotional support for those long days, longer weeks and dreary months.

In all this, their most trusted friend was Miep Gies.
Like the Prank family, she not a native to Amsterdam. She

was born in Vienna in 1909; when the First World War began, she was five. Under a program designed to shelter children from war, she was sent by train to the Netherlands. Her temporary stay was extended, then extended again. She slowly began a new life, a new language, new friends, a new school.

Her real first name was Hermine, Hermine Santrouschitz, but the Dutch family who adopted her, the Nieuwenhuises, began calling her by a Dutch nickname. Miep.

In 1933, she was 24, and fully capable of working outside the home. A friend advised her of a job opportunity working with Otto Frank. He had come recently from Frankfurt, so recently that his wife and children hadn't yet arrived.

His was a company that sold pectin to make jams, she learned. When they first met, he led her to a kitchen; for two weeks she made jam and more jam and more jam, until she understood the process. She asked him to call her Miep.

After two weeks she was led to a desk in the front office. She was assigned to the Complaint and Information desk, where she routinely took calls from housewives who didn't quite understand the instructions on how to use the company's pectin and make jams.

Otto Frank soon asked her to stay on as a regular employee and also soon she met his wife and youngest daughter Anne, who was four at the time and didn't know Dutch, only German. And she later met Margot.

And she met Henk Gies, a few years older than she. They were eventually married.

She was invited to join a Nazi Girl's Club; she refused because of what the Nazis were doing to Jews in Germany.

When she and Henk had been married one year, they were invited to a wedding celebration in the *Het Achterhuis,* as Anne had christened it, or *The Annex,* also her term.

She quickly became, in fact, the most trusted guest—and friend—in *The Annex.*

She kept the eight informed of increasing *razias,* raids, or Nazi round-ups, of all the Jews they could find.

And, she said, it was Otto Frank's idea to set up the bookcase to conceal the door to the *Het Achterhuis.*

And thieves were everywhere in those days—thieves had broken into the ground floor offices three times—and, as Geis wrote ruefully, if thieves suspected there were Jews at a particular place, they could go to the Nazi police. The thieves were financially rewarded by the Nazis and the Jews got caught. (At first the Nazis paid 7.50 guilders for each Jew turned over to them, but they later raised the amount to 25 guilders to make these betrayals more attractive.)

Melissa Müller describes the Secret Annex in detail in her book *Anne Frank: The Biography,* from the top floor down. The first day was Monday July 6, 1942:

> Once Miep closed the door to the annex behind them, the world outside disappeared, shrunk to a memory. Their world had shrunk to a little less than fifty square meters. On the third floor of the annex were two small rooms, stuffy and damp, one no more than three meters wide and five long, with massive ceiling beams that seemed to press down on the little room and squeeze the air out of it. It would be Otto and Edith Frank's living room and bedroom. The other room was considerably narrower, only as wide as its window. It would have to do for Anne and Margot. The bathroom, accessible both from Anne and Margo's room and from the hallway, was spartan but at least included a washbasin with running water—only cold, unfortunately—and a separate toilet,

which could not be flushed during business hours. The water and sewer pipes ran down inside a wall adjacent to one of the storerooms on the first floor. The flushing of the toilet could be heard by anyone below.

A dizzyingly steep staircase led to the Annex's largest room, which contained kitchen cabinets, a stove, and a sink and had originally served as a kind of laboratory for Pectacon. Off this room was a tiny room with a window opening onto the interior courtyard. This cramped space was no more than a little vestibule or passageway; the stairs leading the attic left barely enough room for a narrow bed and a very small table.

This cubbyhole would be a bedroom for Peter Van Pels, who with his parents and his cat Mouchi, would join the Franks in the annex a week later on July 13. During the day the large room would be available to everyone in the annex and a kind of common room; at night it would be the van Pelses' bedroom.

Four adults, three near-adults and Peter's black cat that he brought along despite a prior agreement that he would not—seven people and a cat in rooms as small as prison cells, in fifty square meters that were hot and stuffy in the summer because the windows always had to stay closed, and bone-chillingly cold in the winter because the coal stove often failed to supply enough heat, Under no circumstances would Anne and the others be able to go outdoors. Their only "outings" would be to the attic where, standing back at a safe distance from a large closed window, they could look out into the back yards of neighboring buildings and onto the crown of a huge chestnut tree that let them watch the seasons change.

Once the office workers had left for the day, the eight could venture downstairs, wander around the larger rooms and even play a radio, softly. But not go outside.

Among the trunks, suitcases and boxes of stuff brought to the Secret Annex, Anne's father found her collection of Hollywood clippings. Anne loved everything about Hollywood: the stars; their biographies and stories; and all American films. He suggested she paste the clippings beside her bed— to establish a small sense of normality. She did so, happily.

A family friend, Victor Kugler, brought her movie magazines, from the outside.

Otto Frank took control of decisions made in the Secret Annex, politely but firmly. Others, probably Anne and Margot, called him the Prussian Officer. He should have been exempt from Nazi reprisals; he had won the Iron Cross for Germany in World War I. The same medal had been awarded to Adolph Hitler, who had been gassed and wounded during World War I, and who wore it proudly on his Nazi uniforms. Except Otto Frank was Jewish.

They became *onderduiker* (undergounders), those who lived in hiding.

And they sometimes called their hiding plane the *orphanage*.

Melissa Müller writes that their hiding was not, in fact, unusual: "Of the Jews living in Holland between 1942 and 1943, twenty thousand and perhaps as many as thirty thousand— the estimates vary widely—saw going into hiding as their only alternative to deportation. But the way the Franks went into hiding was by no means typical. Most families separated, with the parents entrusting their children to the care of organized resistance groups. They drummed new family names into the children's heads, names that didn't sound Jewish, and arranged for them live with people who—at least to the children—were utter strangers."

And, she writes, "Very few of those who went into hiding could rely on the kind of loyal, well-organized team of helpers the Franks had, selfless people who they had known for years and who not only provided them with essentials but also stood by them as friends, even bringing them gifts on their birthdays and on holidays."

Their new life in the *Het Achterhuis*, seemed to Anne, as she wrote in her diary on July 11, 1942, "more like being on vacation in a very peculiar pension." (guest house or boardinghouse.)

On vacation in a very peculiar boardinghouse, indeed.

Then the denouement. On August 4, 1945, the Gestapo Department IV B4, the Jewish Division, Amsterdam, got a call. Several Jews apparently were hiding at 263 Prinsengracht. The voice talking to the Gestapo was very precise; the informant sounded legitimate. The Gestapo sent SS Oberscharführer Karl Silberbauer and other Gestapo agents to the address.

Who was the informant? One name was William Gerard van Maaren, who worked on the ground floor. When the offices were empty, those upstairs came down to the second floor and often listened to the radio, for news of the war. One night Hermann van Pels lost his wallet while downstairs; van Maaren later found it. What would a wallet be doing there, when supposedly no one was in the offices after hours? There was money in the wallet; van Maaren kept the money but gave the wallet to Victor Kruger, who had officially taken Otto Frank's position in the firm.

Anne Frank thought him a suspect long before. In her diary entry Thursday, September 16, 1943, she wrote: "Another fact that doesn't exactly brighten our days is that Mr. van Maaren, the man who works in the warehouse, is getting suspicious about the Annex."

van Maaren became a snoop—looking through windows, leaving flour on the floor so he could find footprints. And his suspicions never faded. The lost wallet, found downstairs when no one should have been there, may have been the key to the betrayal.

Did van Maaren call the Gestapo? Or did someone else? Some neighbors in the area may have been suspicious too. The name of the informant scarcely mattered.

Of the eight in hiding, only one survived the rest of the war and came back alive.

The Diary

When Otto Frank was released from Auschwitz by Russian liberators, he and others were put on a train to the Polish city of Katowice. There he got his first bath in months, new clothes and decent meals. He also met an acquaintance, Rootje de Winter, who had been in the Westerbork transit camp at the time time.

Frank asked about his wife.

Dead in Auschwitz, he was told. Sent to the hospital unit, which gave *no hospital help*, she died of starvation and exhaustion. Frank put his head on the table without saying a word.

On a ship from Odessa enroute to Marseille, he wrote:

> My entire hope lies with the children. I cling to the conviction that they are alive and that we'll be together again, but I'm not promising myself anything. We have all experienced too much to pin our hopes on that kind of thing. Only the children count. *Only the children* count."

He took a train across France and arrived in Amsterdam June 3, 1945.

(A similar story: Primo Levi was an Italian Jew swept up in the Nazi juggernaut when he was 14 or 15. He later said he lost his innocence in the cattle cars, taking him and others to the death camps. He was 15 or perhaps 16 when he entered Auschwitz. He got the tattoo 174517 and became a *Häftling*. A prisoner. He spent 11 months as a prisoner, until the Russians liberated Auschwitz. Of 650 Jews in that camp, he was one of 20 who survived. He finally was able to return to Italy wearing the only clothes he had: a Russian army uniform. He later wrote *If This Is a Man* (1947). It became one of the major books about the Holocaust. (His book was rejected in the U.S by publisher Little, Brown on the advise of Rabbi Joshua Liebman.)

Otto Frank immediately went to Miep Gies's apartment. She met him at the door. There were no words between the two of them. He stayed as a guest of Miep and her husband for seven years.

The next day he went to Prinsengracht 263; the Secret Annex was empty, desolate, debris on the floors.

During that period, he wrote to his own mother:

> Everything is like a strange dream. In reality, I can't sort myself out yet … I don't know where the children are, but I never stop thinking of them.

A month later, on July 18, 1945, he read Red Cross fatalities lists and discovered the names Annelies Marie Frank and Margot Betti Frank, with crosses next to each name.

Gone.

He traced who had reported the names to the Red Cross and found two survivors of Auschwitz, two sisters, Lin and Janny Brilleslijper. Those sisters had seen Anne and Margot at a water pipe, in Auschwitz, wearing only blankets. (They had thrown their clothes away, totally infected with lice, which cause typhus.)

In *The Diary That Changed the World,* Karen Bartlett quotes them as saying (emphasis added):

"They looked like little frozen birds."

A few days later Margot could not speak due to a high fever. Anne said, "Here we can lie together and be at peace."

Margot died first, then Anne.

The two sisters carried the dead little birds to mass graves for burial. The camp was liberated by the Allies three weeks later.

Rose of Sharon's still-born baby toward the end of *The Grapes of Wrath*. The two little frozen dead birds.

Who cannot say they are the same?

Their father said he would never be able to bear the reality of his children's deaths.

Miep Geis found Anne's diary in the debris of the deserted Secret Annex. She did not give it immediately to Otto Frank; she too, expected that Anne would return and that Anne would give it to her father.

Anne was so secretive about her diary that her father had never read it in the months they had spent together in the Secret Annex.

Miep Geis finally gave it to him. Otto Frank had remarried. He had lost his wife and daughters. Fritzi Geiringer had lost hers. They lived in Amsterdam and later moved to Basel. He took the diary to his stepdaughter Eva's house (Eva Geiringer) to read, for the first time.

> He read slowly, but he was trembling and couldn't get far without breaking down in tears. He was astonished by the daughter he discovered in the pages, an Anne he did not recognize with deep thoughts and feelings about the world, she later said.

Her father might have suspected her diary would be all about teenaged boys and Hollywood movie stars, but she wrote with wisdom and clarity and offered mature observations and insights, and some humor, laughing at others and often laughing at herself.

Simply stated: her diary kept him alive.

Every detail in her life in the Secret Annex gave him a reason to continue.

"I read on and on," he said in late September 1946, in a letter to his mother, living in Switzerland and distant relatives there. "I can't explain it to you! "

And later he added:

"I can't put Anne's diary down, it's so astonishing … I don't want it out of my hands for a moment …"

Perhaps without realizing it, he was editing it slightly for publication.

He carefully reviewed the text, cutting out some references to Anne's mother, some he thought too hurtful. Anne had made some revisions to her original entries; the originals became version A, the revisions became version B and her Father's revisions or additions, version C.

He believed the diary should be published in German, in Germany, as a tool for teaching German children about the hatred for the Jews and the Holocaust, but some friends and acquaintances believed it would make little difference in Germany, in those post-war years.

Initial reactions to possible publication were decidedly negative: the firm Querido rejected it; publisher Gottfried Bermann Fisher of the publishing firm S. Fisher Verlag, rejected it as did the firm Blast.

He then thought to take out the German phrases, recently added. Then, as sometimes happens, a friend of a friend of a friend helped.

He gave the manuscript to Werner Cahn, who passed it along to Annie Romein-Verschoor, who gave it to her husband Jan Romein, a noted Dutch historian.

He wrote an article for the newspaper *Het Parool, (The Watchword)* which had been allied with the Dutch resistance during the war. His article appeared on the front page April 3, 1946, under the headline "A Child's Voice."

He wrote, in part:

> By chance a diary written during the war years has come into my possession. The Netherlands State Institute for War Documentation already holds some similar diaries, but I should be very much surprised if there were another as lucid, as intelligent, and the same time as natural.

The publisher Contact became interested. But one of their executives, G. P. De Neve, was a staunch Catholic and objected to passages about Anne's menstruation, her interest in a young female friend's breasts and her dislike of her mother.

Otto Frank had to negotiate and re-negotiate these points, a task he had to endure again and again as the diary was published by various publishing firms.

Eventually 25 passages were removed from the dairy, as it went into book form. It was sanitized … before publication.

A review in the newspaper *De Groene Amsterdammer (The Green Amsterdammer)* complimented:

... the intelligence, the honesty, the insight with which she observed herself and her surroundings, and the talent with which she was able to depict what she saw.

And yet, detractors: Rabbi Awraham Soetendorp told Otto Frank, "There was no point in publishing as no one would be interested in the diary." (Think again of the U.S. publisher who rejected George Orwell's *Animal Farm*: "Americans don't buy books about animals," and the U.S. rejection of Primo Levi's memoir.)

Others in the Amsterdam Jewish community—and Jewish communities elsewhere—were equally skeptical or downright negative. In general, the complaints, or criticisms, were:

- The Frank family surely didn't represent typical Jewish families caught in the Holocaust. Few other families would have the resources or the facilities for their own Secret Annex;
- The war was almost an afterthought. Anne's diary entries were written entirely inside the Secret Annex;
- She cast herself as the innocent victim, without the ability to defend herself. At 13, 14 and 15, it seemed a logical thought but others, later, didn't fully accept her rationale.

Following the publication of Anne's diary by the firm Contact, Otto traveled to Paris and arranged the publication in French by the firm Calmann-Lévy, which released it in August 1950. Karen Bartlett writes the book was released "to great critical acclaim and commercial success," but here the trouble began.

A friend of a friend of a friend ...

"One French reader," Bartlett writes, passed, the book to her husband, Meyer Levin. He was a novelist and had been a war correspondent and had written about the death camps.

In England, the firm Secker and Warburg rejected publication; they were the publisher of George Orwell's two best-known books *Animal Farm* and *1984* and should have recognized the value of *The Diary* ... but didn't.

Meyer Levin believed himself the only person to negotiate for, and represent *The Diary* ... ignoring, or bypassing, Otto Frank. Bartlett writes:

> Levin told friends he believed Anne Frank was the "teller" for the story of the Jews of Europe and wrote to Otto to offer his services in translating and selling the book around the world. "My interest in the diary is not commercial so much as one of sympathy and I would be glad of the opportunity translate it."

The firm Contact was negotiating with other publishers around the world; a relatively common practice in publishing.

The British edition was published by the firm Valentine Mitchell, but their managing director, David Kessler, said, "The fact that it records war-time experiences is, to my mind, far less important than its qualities as a remarkable document of a girl's adolescence."

That was the core of the dilemma: was it a Holocaust document, a war-time document or simply a diary of the adolescence of a young girl?

It was, in truth, simply all three.

It did not sell well in England; the publisher printed 5,000 copies, but sales were slow. By late 1951 the, firm decided that the run of *The Diary* . . . was at its end. They did not authorize a second printing and the book went out-of -print in England thereafter.

Sales were also slow in the original Contact edition and Otto Frank feared that it too, would go out-of-print.

Then … the breakthrough.

Following publication in England, Otto Frank began to set his sights on publication in America.

Results initially, were the same as elsewhere—some publishers had little interest, others had no interest at all.

The project was rejected: by Appleton Century; Harper; Harcourt; Alfred Knopf; Shocken, which published a variety of Judaica titles; Scribner's; Simon and Schuster; Vanguard and Viking—all rejected it. A reader at Knopf thought it " a dreary record of typical family bickering, petty annoyances and adolescent emotions." Random House was a maybe.

Little, Brown and Doubleday remained in the hunt. (Staff people at the Paris offices of Doubleday had rescued a copy in the "slush pile" of projects due to be rejected.)

The contract was eventually won by Doubleday. Four staff members at Doubleday: Frank Price, Jason Epstein, Karen Rye and Barbara Zimmerman formed an "Informal Society of Advocates for Anne Frank."

Zimmerman was the foremost of the four. If Anne Frank had lived she and Zimmerman would have been the same age. Zimmerman was the one who thought to involve Eleanor Roosevelt in the project. Eventually, Roosevelt "wrote" a short Introduction, but the first draft was probably written by Zimmerman, then only approved by Roosevelt, to be used in her name.

Zimmerman and Otto Frank became close and remained close for decades.

Enter Meyer Levin again.

In journalism, the top of any nonfiction article is called the lead, pronounced *leed*. Usually three paragraphs, it summarizes the article, so if a reader doesn't have the time to read through the complete article, the lead is enough to tell the story. There are 26 different techniques for writing the lead, from simple and easy to use, to more complicated and rarely seen, but in any case, it should be appropriate to the article (the story) and have impact.

Levin contributed an essay to *The New York Times Book Review* June 15, 1952. *The Times* was, and is, the leading source of major book reviews in this country.

His lead was:

Anne Frank's diary is too tenderly intimate a book to be foreseen with the label "classic," and yet no lesser designation serves. For little Anne Frank, spirited, moody, self-doubting, succeeded in communicating in virtually perfect, or classic, form the drama of puberty. But her book is not a classic to be left on the library shelf. It is a warm and stirring confession, to be read over and over for insight and enjoyment …

There is no lugubrious ghetto tale, no compilation of horrors. Reality can prove surprisingly different from invented reality, and Anne Frank's diary simply bubbles with amusement, love, discovery. It has its share of disgust, its moments of hatred, but it is so wondrously alive, so near, that one feels overwhelmingly true universalities of human nature. These people might be living next door; their within-the-family emotions, their tensions and satisfactions are those of human character and growth, anywhere.

"I want to go on living even after my death," Anne wrote … There is anguish in the thought of how much creative power, how much sheer beauty of living, was cut off through genocide. But through her diary Anne goes on living.

His essay was spot-on accurate.

It ignited interest in the book throughout America, and indeed, echoed throughout the world.

Barbara Zimmerman said "The review itself is a beautiful one … It was damn good, very dramatic and really hit hard. It struck a chord with people and made them race out to read the diary."

Levin wrote a second essay, published in the Jewish *Congress Weekly*, and claimed the book was the most important document to have come out of the "great catastrophe." The Holocaust, he wrote, had, at long last, come home, "and our defenses are shattered. We weep."

The Diary of a Young Girl, published by Doubleday, went on sale June 16, 1952. All 5,000 copies were sold that day. (This was, of course, decades before internet book sales. Amazon was founded in 1994 by Jeff Bezos—originally to sell books.)

Doubleday ordered a second printing of 15,000 copies.

Within two years, 80,000 hardcover and 200,000 paperback copies were sold.

And yet, Levin's arguments with, and an animosity toward, Otto Frank, went on for years. In fact, they never abated.

There was a major renaissance among American Jewish communities in the post-war years and Anne Frank was the center, as Karen Bartlett writes, in *The Diary That Changed the World:*

Invariably, the first book Jewish groups bought was *The Diary of Anne Frank*—her innocent face, those big eyes, her family background and her dreams for her future melding so perfectly with the American dream of that era. The real life-and-death battles of the Jewish ghetto fighters of Poland made Americans feel uncomfortable with vivid descriptions of the blood, gore and poverty in East European Jewish life—but Anne Frank offered the perfect antidote. A story of a middle-class girl from a loving nuclear family who enjoyed wholesome vigorous activities was the kind of tale most Americans enjoyed watching at the movie. Anne was a sort of Jewish Velvet Brown from *National Velvet,* who went ice-skating instead of horse-riding, bought pretty dresses, rode her bicycle and had birthday parties. She was feisty and fought her mother. She liked boys. But undoubtedly, she was a good girl who could always rely on the wise counsel of her father. As the editors at Doubleday had rightly realized, Anne's positive message for the future and uplifting ending was crucial.

And, the most important quotation from her beliefs and the most often quoted from *The Diary* ... is:

"In spite of everything I still think people are really good at heart. "
— July 15, 1944 entry, page 332 in Otto Frank—Miriam Pressler, *The Diary of a Young Girl: The Definitive Edition.*

This was eventually used as the end quotation in the stage-play of the book.

The reach of her book was almost universal. In her essay "Teaching Anne Frank in the US," Hana Abramovitch writes:

> Anne's diary has a singular place in American education. Adopted by teachers within few years of it is publication in English translation, it soon became the first widely taught text about a victim of the Holocaust. *The Diary of a Young Girl* also became the most widely read work written by an adolescent girl.

And, as Karen Bartlett writes,

> Within thirty years, half of all American high-school students had *The Dairy of Anne Frank* on their required reading list, with most first encountering it in class at age twelve—just younger than Anne when she wrote it.

The Play

Editors at Doubleday asked Otto Frank if they could negotiate the theatrical rights for the Diary, for a standard ten percent commission. He agreed, with the stipulation that Meyer Levin be given approval rights. Doubleday agreed that Levin would be given half their commission.

So far everyone was satisfied. But soon, Barbara Zimmerman, at Doubleday, believed that Levin was "impossible to deal with on any terms, officially, legally, morally, personally," and claimed, "he seemed intent on destroying both himself and Anne's play."

Francine Prose writes that, as the book version soared into the best-seller strata, there were others needed for the stage version:

Famous writer. Important playwright. Or sometimes more coarsely, *big name.* The big names bandied about included Arthur Miller, Lillian Heilman, Thornton Wilder, Maxwell Anderson, Harold Churman, Elia Kazan, and Joshua Logan.

Lists were published; none of them included Meyer Levin.

Levin insisted that no one be allowed to write the theatrical version if they were not Jewish, a stipulation that offended Otto Frank.

He replied:

I always said that Anne's book is not a warbook. War is in the background. It is not a Jewish book either, though Jewish sphere, sentiment and surrounding is the background. I never wanted a Jew writing an introduction for it. It is (at least here) read and understood more by gentiles than in Jewish circles.

I do not know how that will be in the USA, it is the case in Europe. So do not make a Jewish play out of it! In some way of course it must be Jewish, even so that it works against anti-Semitism. I do not know if I can express what I mean and only hope that you won't misunderstand.

Levin was not mollified; the people at Doubleday, on the other hand, began to simply ignore him, He claimed that everyone was conspiring against him—a Communist cabal of sorts, somehow, including, among others, Lillian Hellman.

In a key encounter, Francine Prose writes, Hellman told Garson Kanin that the stage play needed a lighter touch. Emphasize Anne's humor, she said. And Kermit Bloomgarden had said the same. "Get (the audience) laughing. . . That way, it's possible for them to sit through the show."

Levin wrote his own version of the stageplay. It was, Francine Prose writes,

> Dark. Depressive, Jewish, Gloomy. Insufficiently *universal*. The polar opposite of *commercial*.

Kermit Bloomgarden agreed to produce the play.

The team of Frances Goodrich and Albert Hackett became prime candidates to write the script. They had success the past with scripts for *Seven Brides for Seven Brothers; The Virginian; The Thin Man, Easter Parade* and *Father of the Bride,* which, Francine Prose writes, showed they could write about adolescents.

When Meyer Levin heard about Bloomgarden and the Goodrich-Hackett team, he paid for an advertisement in *The New* Vork *Post.* It perfectly revealed Levin's compulsion—fixation—obsession.

> A challenger to Kermit Bloomgarden.
> Is it right for you, to kill a play that others find deeply moving, and are eager to produce?
> When you secured the stage rights to Anne Frank's *Diary of a Young Girl* you knew I had already dramatized the book, but you approved new adapters ... and shoved my play aside. The Diary is dear to many hearts, yours, mine, and the public's. There is a responsibility to see that what may be the right adaption is not cast away.

It went on as such for six more paragraphs; it is the very definition of a rant:

Levin wrote to Otto Frank: since he—Levin and Anne—were both writers, he was the only person to interpret her work. Otto Frank, as her father, was out of this equation, Levin insisted.

Levin's rant in *The New York Post* was the end of the line; Otto. Frank had been cordial with Levin in the past, but no more.

The Goodrich-Hackett duo went through eight versions of the playscript; some too ponderous, others too unsympathetic to the characters. Francine Prose writes that they sent their fourth version to Bloomgarden and Lillian Hellman and both hated it.

The production crew could have found a European actress to play Anne; that would have given the play a layer of cachet. Instead they Americanized it, using Susan Strasberg in that role. The play opened October 5, 1956 at the Cort Theater in New York and was directed by Garson Kanin. It was moved to the Ambassador Theater in February, 1957; it played, in New York for 717 performances; the troupe then traveled throughout the United States with Millie Perkins playing the Anne Frank role.

It received a Tony award for Best Play; Susan Strasberg was nominated for Best Actress; and it received nominations, for Best Scenic Design, Best Costume Design and and Best Director.

It received a Pulitzer Prize for Drama for the Goodrich—Hackett writing team.; Susan Strasberg won the 1956 Theater World Award and the play received the 1956 New York Drama Critics Circle ward for best play.

The Film

The film version soon followed. Millie Perkins was again cast as Anne Frank and Joseph Schildkraut again played the role of Otto Frank. The rest of the cast were new to this production.

George Stevens directed the film version.

Otto Frank initially asked Audrey Hepburn if she would play Anne Frank. Hepburn and Anne Frank were born witHin a month of each other and both spent their adolescent years in Holland under Nazi rule. Hepburn eventually declined, stating, at that time, she thought she was too old for the role.

It was released March 18, 1959.

The film was nominated in a wide variety of categories for a total of nine Academy Awards. Shelly Winters won Best Supporting Actress for her role as Mrs. Van Daan; she donated her award to the Anne Frank House in Amsterdam, where it is on display. The film won best Art Direction for a black-and-white film. It was nominated for six Golden Globe awards

The film was re-released in DVD and Blu-ray versions February 3,2004; that date was chosen because some believed that would have been Anne Frank's 80th birthday. These versions are still available in new and used copies across the internet and elsewhere.

Various editions of *The Diary of a Young Girl* continue to sell, world-wide.

Anne Frank and
The Grapes of Wrath

John Steinbeck, 1939

In the 1930s, John Steinbeck began writing a novel, about migrants—Okies—in California. He called it *L'Affair Lettuceberg*; it didn't work, didn't jell. He abandoned it, and began again, with a new subject and a new title, *The Grapes of Wrath*, a title suggested to him by his wife, ("tramping out the vintage where the grapes of wrath are stored," from *The Battle Hymn of the Republic* by Julia Ward Howe. Lyrics appear on the end papers of the 50th anniversary edition of *Grapes … .)*

It is, in fact, a retelling of the biblical Tribe of Israel, leaving their Land of Bondage and journeying toward their Promised Land.

Steinbeck wrote it—beginning to end—in 100 days, a sprint, not a marathon, and it very nearly gave him a nervous breakdown. (Few major novels are ever deliberately written in such short time span.)

The Grapes of Wrath is rife with biblical references, but they—almost all—are black reversals of the biblical stories.

Examples:

A preacher, Jim Casy —initials J.C.—travels with the Joads from Oklahoma to California. In California he is shot by vigilantes—government thugs. His dying words:
"You don't know what you're doin.'"
Christ on the Cross:
"Forgive them Father, they know not what they do."
(Luke 23:34)

A young woman, Rose of Sharon (a biblical name) is pregnant throughout the trek from Oklahoma to California with the Joads. Her husband deserts her and disappears along the way. She gives birth in a boxcar in California during a flood. But she has had no adequate nutrition along the way and the baby is stillborn. Born dead. What to do? The Joads take the lifeless body from her and find a crate used to pack apples. They put the body in the crate and push it into the nearest river. "Go downstream and show them what happened to you." Meaning: local citizens who might find the body in the crate would know it was an Okie baby which could not legally be buried in a California cemetery.

What biblical story is this?

A black reversal of the joy of those who found the baby Moses in the bullrushes along a river. (Exodus 1:15-22)

Near the end of the novel, the son, Tom Joad, has to tell his mother he is leaving the family; he has a criminal record in their native state of Oklahoma and if he is caught—for any reason or for no reason at all—the family might well be dragged into an ugly mess.

His mother, Ma Joad, with all the heartbreak of any mother, anywhere, says, "Where ya gonna be, Tommy?"

" ... I'll be around in the dark. I'll be ever' where—wherever you look. Wherever they's a fight so hungry people can eat, I'll be there. Wherever they's a cop beatin' up a guy, I'll be there. If Casy knowed, why, I'll be in the way kids yell when they're mad an'—I'll be in the way kids laugh when they're hungry an' they know supper's ready. An' when our folks eat the stuff they raise an' live in the houses they build, why, I'll be there."

The biblical reference?

The Lord: "Lo, I will be with you always." (Mathew 18:20)

Estimates are that one million people migrated to California during The Great Depression years from midwest states: Oklahoma, Kansas and others in the American heartland. California simply could not absorb all this extra workforce. They were called derisively—Okies—and prejudice was rampart. They were treated worse there than in their former states.

Steinbeck's *The Grapes of Wrath* was first published April 14, 1939. It has become *the* premier novel of the Depression Years.

Steinbeck may have wanted to eventually settle along Monterey Bay—with a view of the Pacific. He became widely hated in California, especially among big growers and big banks. He never returned to live in his native state; he eventually settled in Sag Harbor, Long Island—with a view of the Atlantic. (There is a statue of him now in his hometown of Salinas, California. For unaccountable reasons it appears less than life- size, making him look like a troll or a Hummel figure.)

The Great Depression finally ended in a way no could have anticipated: when Japan attacked Pearl Harbor, December 7, 1941, America entered the Second World War. Suddenly everyone was needed; men and women entered the armed forces in huge numbers, armament plants and other war plants were established suddenly throughout the country. By the end of the war, everyone was needed and everyone was assimilated. Or nearly so.

Would Anne Frank have known about *The Grapes of Wrath?* Not likely. Publication in the United States in 1939 would have meant that early copies would not have reached Amsterdam before Anne and the others closed the bookcase door and lived for two years-plus in the Secret Annex.

But would she have appreciated The *Grapes of Wrath … ?*

A caveat and a question here—if she had read an early copy of *The Grapes of Wrath* in the Secret Annex, as part of a Jewish family, would she have understood Steinbeck's subtle references to the Christian Bible? Probably not -- would she have a clear idea of the plight of the Okies—a plight only in lesser degrees to her own?

Surely so.

Steinbeck's Joad family was fictional, but he knew real-life Joads who had migrated into his native California from the midwest.

Re-reading *The Diary of a Young Girl* and *The Grapes of Wrath* concurrently means that Anne and Margot Frank and her parents and the others in the Secret Annex and the others throughout Nazi-occupied Europe—all the countless, nameless others—were all Joads, but to the n th degree worse, in the 1930s and 1940s.

The End

The Nazis captured all eight in the Secret Annex on August 4, 1944.

All eight were transferred from a prison in Amsterdam to the Westerbork transit camp in northeast Holland. They were then placed on the last transport train from there to Auschwitz.

Hermann van Pels was killed in the Auschwitz gas chambers sometime in October or November, 1944; the gas chambers were demolished shortly thereafter.

Auguste van Pels, his wife, was transferred from Auschwitz to Bergen-Belsen, then to Buchenwald, then to Theresienstadt on April 9, 1945. She may have been transferred elsewhere; her death location and date of death are not known.

Peter van Pels, their son, was forced to take part in a "death march" on January 16, 1945, from Auschwitz to Mauthausen, in Austria; he died there May 5, 1945, three days before that camp was liberated.

Fritz Pfeffer, the dentist (Albert Dussel in Anne's diary entries), died in the Neuengamme concentration camp, December 10, 1944, after he had been transferred there from either Buchenwald or Sachsenhausen.

Edith Frank, Anne and Margot's mother, died in Auschwitz-Birkenau, January 6, 1945, from starvation and exhaustion.

Otto Frank, their father, was in Auschwitz when it was liberated by Russian troops. He retuned to Amsterdam by way of Odessa and Marseille, arriving June 1, 1945.

He was the only one of eight from the Secret Annex who survived.

Anne and Margot were transferred from Auschwitz to Bergen-Belsen, a concentration camp, at the end of October, 1944. Typhus, spread by lice, erupted in an epidemic during the winter of 1944-1945, killing hundreds and hundreds of prisoners. The Nazis didn't care if prisoners died of disease or starvation; their bodies were burned day-by-day in mass piles.

Margot Frank died of typhus there in February or March, 1945. Anne died soon after.

British troops liberated the camp April 12, 1945.

Inma Sonneberg Merkel had the same experiences as the Franks. Like them, she was Jewish, born in Germany, married and had two children. When Hitler came to power, they fled to Holland. They were able to send one child out of the country and the other to her sister for hiding in The Hague.

She and her husband were caught and sent to Westerbork in 1942; a year later they were sent to Bergen-Belsen. Her husband and a brother died there. She survived for three years and was there when the camp was liberated in the spring of 1945.

In 1977, with the help of Jonathan Alter, then at *Newsweek*, she wrote a short memoir, about Bergen-Belsen, published in the July 21, 1977 issue. She was 100 the April before.

In part, she wrote:

One of the children in my barracks toward the end of the war was Anne Frank, whose diary became famous after her death. I didn't know her family beforehand, and I don't recall much about her, but I do remember her as a quiet child. When I heard later she was 15 when she was in the camp, I was surprised. She seemed younger to me. Pen and paper were hard to find, but I have a memory of her writing a bit. Typhus was a terrific problem, especially for the children. Of 500 in my barracks, maybe 100 got it and most of them died. Many others starved to death. When Anne Frank got sick with typhus, I remember telling her she could stay in the barracks—she didn't have to go to roll call.

There was so little to eat. In my early days there, we were each given one roll of bread for eight days, and we tore it up, piece by piece. One cup of black coffee a day and one cup of soup. And water. That was all. Later there was even less. When I asked the commandant for a little bit of gruel for the children's diet, he would sometimes give me extra cereal. But how could I find cereal for her? It was only for the little children and only a little bit. The children died anyway. A couple of trained nurses were among the inmates, and they reported to me. In the evening, we tried help the sickest. In the morning, it was part of my job to tell the soldiers how many had died the night before. Then they would throw the bodies on the fire.

I have a dim memory of Anne Frank speaking of her father. She was a nice, fine person. She would say to me "Irma, I am very sick." I said, "No, you aren't so sick." She wanted to be reassured she wasn't. When she slipped into a coma, I took her in my arms. She didn't know she was dying. She didn't know she was so sick. You never know. At Bergen-Belsen, you didn't not have feelings anymore. You became paralyzed. In all the years since, I almost never talked about Bergen-Belsen.

I couldn't. It was too much.

The headline above her essay:

"I Saw Anne Frank Die"

There is now a simple headstone in the area in Bergen-Belsen where Margot and Anne Frank died.

How many other children like Margot and Anne died in the Holocaust? Estimates range from one million one-and-a-half million. Children.

MARGOT
FRANK
1926-1945
ANNE
FRANK
1929-1945
נר ח' נשמת אדם
(SPRÜCHE 20,27)

Anne Frank and The Road

Cormac McCarthy, 2006

A father and his son are slowly, ever so slowly, traversing a moonscape that is America after a nuclear war. They are heading toward the west coast and the ocean, where they hope to find milder conditions; they don't know how long it will take to get there or if they will ever arrive.

On any day they might succumb slowly to malnutrition, or just as slowly to hypothermia.

All the possessions they own are in an old grocery cart which they push on roads, or often on no roads. The going is painstakingly slow, the cart awkward.

The father was married; his wife gave birth to the son, but later died, a suicide.

They are always on the lookout for anyone else on the road; any stranger might be an enemy; in fact, the father once had to kill a stranger who was attempting to kidnap the son. Strangers might possibly even be cannibals.

They investigate every house they see standing; in a mansion deserted—*for how many years or decades?*—they discover a trove of canned goods, a godsend for them. The trek goes on and on, ever so slowly, the narrative made special by Cormac McCarthy's prose. The dialogue between father and son is always thus, much of it biblical in its simplicity and intimate (and without standard punctuation):

> He woke in the night and lay listening. He couldn't remember where he was. The thought made him smile.
>
> Where are we, he said.
> What is it Papa?
> Nothing. We're okay. Go to sleep.
> We're going to be okay, aren't we Papa?
> Yes. We are.
> And nothing bad is going to happen to us.
> That's right.
> Because we are carrying the fire.
> Yes. Because we are carrying the fire.

In the early 2000s, McCarthy and his son were staying in a motel in El Paso; he looked out at the mountains and visualized that city after an apocalyptic war. He jotted two pages of notes and kept them; four years later while living in Ireland, he wrote *The Road*. In it, many of the conversations between father and son were actual conversations McCarthy remembered with his own son.

It has become one of the most acclaimed novels in recent years.

In this section, he describes how they found the remnants of cannibalism:

> They walked into the little clearing, the boy clutch-ing his hand. They'd taken everything with them except whatever black thing was skewered over the coals. He

was standing there checking the perimeter when the boy turned and buried his face against him. What is it? he said. What is it? The boy shook his head. Oh Papa, he said. He turned and looked again. What the boy had seen was a charred human infant headless and gutted and blackened on the spit. He bent down and picked the boy up and started for the road with him. Holding him close. I'm sorry, he whispered. I'm sorry.

The narrative is relentless in its simplicity; it is *haunting, harrowing* and *hypnotic.*

The denouement won't be revealed here (or *wont be,* as McCarthy would write it), but suffice to say it is a triumph of the human spirit and the universal will to continue.

And what of Anne Frank? *The Road* was published in 2006; she died in 1945.

Let us suppose, just for a moment, that the nurse/inmates in Bergen-Belsen were able to hold her typhus in check, that she would survive until the war was over, just a few weeks away.

And that she could regain her health, however slowly that might have been.

She would have had to return to Amsterdam, by a wandering route, the type of route her father had to take.

Substitute *post-war Europe,* for *post-apocalyptic America,*

The story remains the same.

The journey of the Joads toward their own promised land in *The Grapes of Wrath.* The journey of the man and his son in *The Road.*

Who cannot say they are the same?

Refugees, survivors, from Nazi concentration camps and death camps, D.P.s they were called. Displaced Persons, hoping to return to their homes, if their homes remained standing. From all over Europe. Trudging to … to where? If their sons and daughters and wives and husbands and parents and relatives and friends still survived. If their towns survived.

If … if … If …

Anne Frank could have written this book either as a European refuge novel, or as nonfiction: real refugees striving to find their way in a new world—the same desperate will to live, in post-war Europe. And surely she would write it with the same life-affirming denouement.

If she had survived.

Anne Frank's Legacy ...
to the World

Since its original publication, *The Diary of a Young Girl* has sold over thirty million copies—30,000,000 copies—world-wide;

The numbers of readers of *The Diary*. . . with pass-along copies read in schools and in public libraries and college and university libraries throughout the world is surely into the untold millions and millions more;

It has been translated into over 70 languages;

Her face is now on postage stamps issued by the Netherlands and other countries. There is statue of her in Amsterdam.

In *Selling the Holocaust,* Tim Cole quotes the editors of *Dutch Holocaust Literature in Historical Perceptive (emphasis added):*

... her face with the sad shy smile is one of the icons of this century, a present-day Mona Lisa.

And, Cole also writes,

Since the 1950s, Anne Frank's name has been attached to a day, a week, a rose, a tulip, countless trees, a whole forest, streets, schools and youth centers, and a village …

There have been over 270 schools named after Anne Frank; 100 in Germany; 89 in France; 45 in Italy; 17 in the Netherlands including a Montessori school which she attended; 4 in Brazil; 4 in the United States; 2 in Bulgaria and one each in Argentina, Belgium, Canada, Columbia, El Salvador, Spain, Hungary, Israel, Nepal, Uruguay and Sweden.

The AnneFrank.org states there are now 1.2 million visitors annually to Amsterdam, from all-around the world, to visit the Secret Annex …

Stated quite simply: *The Diary of a Young Girl*—and her life story—has become one of the most consequential of the twentieth century.

The Sad, Shy Smile ...

*" ... her face with the sad shy smile
is one of the icons of this century,
a present day–Mona Lisa."*

— Dutch Holocaust Literature in Historical Perspective, 1996.

Anne Frank on postage stamp, The Netherlands, circa 1980.

Emmett Till

Four Steps in America That Changed the World

The Dred Scott Case, 1857

Dred Scott was a slave, born in 1799, who moved with his owner Peter Blow and his family, from Virginia to Alabama, where the Blow family ran a largely unsuccessful farm near Huntsville. (It is not clear whether his name was Dred or a shortened version of Etheldred.)

By 1830, the Blow family gave up farming and moved to St. Louis, Missouri; Scott was sold to Dr. John Emerson, an army surgeon, who planned an Army move to Rock Island, Illinois. Scott attempted to run away, as he disliked Emerson. He dodged capture for a brief period, but was found and returned to Emerson.

In 1836, Emerson was sent to Fort Armstrong, Illinois, a free state, taking Scott with him.

Emerson had further Army postings including, in 1937, at Fort Snelling, now a part of Minnesota. By that time, Dred Scott was married to Harriet Robinson, also a slave. Emerson was then sent to Fort Jessup in Louisiana, also in 1837, leaving the Dred Scott family members in Minnesota and leasing them to others who needed slaves.

The Emersons and the Scott slave family moved to Missouri, a slave state, in 1840. Emerson, the army surgeon, left the Army in 1842 and died in the Iowa Territory that year. His estate, including the slave family, was left to his wife. Dred Scott and his wife had two daughters, Eliza and Lizzie; they also had two sons who died in infancy.

For three years after the surgeon died, his wife continued to lease out the Dred Scott family to others who needed slaves. In 1846, Scott attempted to buy his family out of slavery for $300 (about $9,000. today), but Emerson's widow refused.

Dred Scott was able to sue for his own freedom and the freedom of his wife and their daughters, a lawsuit which became known as the Dred Scott decision.

Dred Scott first filed a lawsuit in the Missouri circuit court, in 1846, arguing that because the Scott family was held for an extended period in a free territory, they had gained their freedom. That doctrine was commonly known as "once free, always free." He and his wife had lived for two years in free states. That court initially ruled in their favor, but their owner appealed; and by 1852 the Missouri Supreme Court decided that slave states did not have to have to abide by laws in free states.

By 1863, Scott was able to file again, this time in federal courts. At this point he had been transferred, as a slave, to the brother of Emersons's widow, a man named John Sanford. His name is misspelled in court records as Sandford.

The case was Scott vs. Sandford.

Supreme Court Chief Justice Roger B. Taney issued the opinion:

1. Any person descending from Africans, whether slave or free, is not a citizen of the United States, according to the United States. Constitution;

2. The Ordinance of 1787 could not confer either freedom or citizenship in the Northwest Territory to non-white individuals:

3. The provisions of the Act of 1820, known as the Missouri Compromise, were voided as a legislative act, since the act exceeds the powers of Congress, insofar as it attempted to exclude slavery and import freedom and citizenship to nonwhite persons in the northern part of the Louisiana purchase.

The Court ruled 7-2 that African Americans had no claim to freedom or citizenship, and as such, had no power to bring a case, or cases, before the court (i.e. they "had no standing").

Taney ruled that because Dred Scott was considered "private property," he was subject to the fifth amendment of the Constitution, which prohibits the taking of property from its owner "without due process."

That case is now widely believed to be the worst case in the history of the Supreme Court; it is based on racism and weak legal reasoning. It only inflamed the widening gap between the north and the south, between free states and slave states. The Civil War began shortly thereafter.

Dred Scott and his family were "manumitted" (given their freedom) by Republican Congressman Taylor Blow, their final owner., in a private ceremony in May 1857. He died the next year.

Dred Scott's legacy to the world:

- In 1957 his gravesite was rediscovered and flowers placed on it to mark the centennial of the case;
- In 1971, Bloomington, Minnesota, dedicated 48 acres as the Dred Scott Playfield;
- In 1977, a National Historic Marker was placed on the Old Courthouse in St.Lous, commemorating the Scott

case. His great-grandson John A. Madison gave the invocation;

- 1997—Dred Scott and Harriet Scott were inducted into the St. Louis Walk of Fame;
- 2001—The petition papers from the Scott case were displayed at the main branch of the St. Louis Public Library, along with papers of more than 300 freedom suits found in the archives of the circuit court;
- 2012—Dred Scott was inducted, into the Hall of Famous Missourians, and a bronze bust is displayed in the Missouri State Capitol Building;
- 2012—A bronze statue of Dred and Harriet Scott was erected outside the Old Courthouse in downtown St. Louis, where their case was originally heard;
- 2017— On the 160th anniversary of when the case was first heard, on the steps of the Maryland State House, near a statue of Supreme Court Court Chief Justice Roger Taney, his great-great-grandnephew Charlie Taney apologized to Scott's great-great-granddaughter Lynne Jackson and to all African- Americans "for the terrible injustice of the Dred Scott decision."

1865-1877—Reconstruction

*" ... with malice toward none,
with charity for all ... "*

—Lincoln's Second Inaugural
March 4, 1865

The 12 years—1865–1877—marked a watershed period in America; in these years nothing less was anticipated than the complete rebuilding of the United States after the Civil War, which cost 620,000 lives (to a new estimate of 750,000 deaths). 620,000 is approximately equal to the total of American fatalities in: the Revolutionary War, the War of 1812, the Mexican War, the Spanish- American War, World War I and World War II combined.

Key principles of Reconstruction were to bring the Confederate States back into the Union and to counteract the social, political and economic effects of slavery during the war years.

Abraham Lincoln and most northern politicians were for Reconstruction; many southern politicians were against it. Although much was accomplished in the vast program's 12 years, it eventually collapsed after Lincoln's assassination when Vice President Andrew Johnson, a southerner, became Lincoln's successor.

Key achievements during these 12 years were:

- Abolishment of slavery;
- Ending the remnants of slavery in the south;
- Passing the 13th, 14th and 15th amendments to the Constitution, collectively known as the Reconstruction

Amendments. Establishing these amendments led—eventually—to a 20th century ruling that outlawed segregated schools. A "Second Reconstruction" in 1964 and 1965 by the Civil Rights movement led to civil rights laws that ended legal segregation and the re-opening of voting to blacks;

- After attacks against Blacks in the South, Congress federalized the protection of civil rights in 1866, placed citizens in formerly Confederate states under the protection of the U.S. military and required those states to guarantee civil rights for freed Black men;

- The Ku Klux Klan had attacked and intimidated southern Blanks, who had attempted to exercise their new civil rights; the Klan also attacked politicians who supported those rights. After the assassination of Republican Congressman James H. Hinds of Arkansas in 1868, President Ulysses S. Grant, who had succeeded Andrew Johnson, suppressed the Ku Klux Klan in 1871.

- Northerners flooded into the south—"Carpetbaggers"— to run Reconstruction programs, to run Southern businesses and perhaps seize them if they could. They, in part and by accident, changed the culture of the South in the post-Civil War years. Against them were the "Redeemers," who wanted to keep as much of the previous South as they could; these included Andrew Johnson, the Klan and others.

And yet . . . and yet. . . and yet. . . Klan attacks continued to occur throughout the former Confederate States;

- Reforms during these years led to a framework for eventual legal rights and legal equity for Blacks.

Reconstruction was far from perfect. Failures during those Reconstruction years included:

- Failures to protect Blacks against the Ku Klux Klan;
- Starvation, brutal treatment and even death among union soldiers during those years;
- Reparations to former slaveowners but not to former slaves
- And following the Reconstruction years:
- The terrors of the Ku Klux Klan, which continued for decades and decades;
- The Jim Crow laws.

The Ku Klux Klan

1865–1872
Birth of a Nation, 1915
1915–1944
1946–present

The white robes, the white hoods—nothing is more symbolic of hatred in America than the Ku Klux Klan.

There have been three versions, or iterations, of the Klan during the years cited above.

The first iteration began just after the Civil War, largely by former Confederate soldiers—they used violence and murder against newly-freed Black people in the south. The origins of the Klan's white hood are largely lost in history; it was used obviously as a disguise—members presumably could not even identify each other, although some could do so by the wearer's mannerisms and speech patterns. Outsiders—enemies of the Klan—could not identify anyone during a few moments of a Klan encounter.

In a remarkable phrase, *The Cyclopaedia of Fraternities,* published in 1907, said

> Beginning in April, 1867, there was a gradual transformation … The members had conjured up a veritable Frankenstein. They had played with an engine of power and mystery, though organized on entirely innocent lines, and found themselves overcome by a belief that something must lie behind it all—that there was, after all, a serious purpose, a work for the Klan to do.

The hoods and cross burnings came into prominence during the second iteration, 1915 -1944.

The first Klan was established in Pulaski, Tennessee in late December, 1865, by six former members of the Confederate army; they sought to restore white supremacy by the use of intimidation, violence and even murder. Their targets were white Northern leaders, freed Black leaders, and other perceived enemies.

Confederate General Nathan Bedford Forrest was elected the first Grand Wizard of the Klan, but despite his election local chapters of the Klan operated independently.

The first iteration of the Klan largely failed because it was not a cohesive organization, and it lost control of the worst among the Klansmen, criminals and others …

By 1870 and 1871, the federal government passed the Enforcement Acts, which were intended to prosecute and suppress the Klan.

The film *Birth of a Nation,* released February, 8, 1915 marked the beginning of the second and most significant iteration of the Klan.

Birth of a Nation is now thought to be the most racist film ever made in Hollywood—it was the first film be shown in the White House, viewed by President Woodrow Wilson and his Cabinet. Wilson himself, is believed to be the most racist president until that dubious distinction was passed to Donald John Trump.

The film was based on the 1905 novel and play *The Clansman,* by Thomas Dixon Jr. Directed by D. W. Griffith, it was innovative and notable for a variety of achievements; it was part historical fact (the assassination of Abraham Lincoln) and part fiction. It chronicled two families; one northern, one southern, and included a variety of techniques then new or never tried:

close-ups; a battle scene with hundreds of extras; a musical score for an orchestra. The film was long enough to have an intermission and had a printed program.

Thomas Dixon's book *The Clansman* included white costumes and the idea of burning crosses, which had not been a part of the first iteration of the Klan.

When the film premiered in Atlanta in December, 1915, William Simmons, who established the second iteration of the Klan at Stone Mountain, Georgia, earlier that same year, attended. Others appeared at the theater in white robes and white hoods; some even rode horses to the theater, to imitate scenes in the film.

The film showed Blacks as unintelligent and aggressive toward white women; many were white actors in blackface.

More importantly, the Ku Klux Klan was portrayed in the film as a necessary force—even a godly force—to protect American values, protect white women and protect white supremacy.

It only inflamed the divides in American culture; the film was the main force in the re-birth of the Klan.

The second iteration of the Klan worked like a business or like a mob family It used paid staff members, had a national headquarters, made profits on sales of robes and hoods and such, and grew through initiation fees paid by new members. It even hired its own publicity company, the Southern Publicity Association.

W. J. Cash, in his 1941 book *The Mind of the South*, includes this remarkable passage (emphasis added). The second Klan was, he said:

> *... anti-Negro, anti-Alien, anti-Red, anti-Catholic, anti-Jew, anti-Darwin, anti-Modern, anti-Liberal ...*

It preached *"One Hundred Percent Americanism."*

Its appeal was exclusively for white Protestants. It not only opposed Jews, Black people, Catholics, but also newly-arriving Southern and Eastern European immigrants such as Italians, Russians and Lithuanias, many of whom were Catholic.

The Klan also opposed homosexuals, Muslims, atheists, and abortion providers.

Mass parades with participants in white robes and hoods were common during this second period; they had not been a part of the first iteration of the Klan.

"White-robed Klan cheered on march in nation's capital"— front-page headline *The Washington Post*, August 9, 1925. More than 30,000 Klan members had marched through Washington, D.C., the day before. As *The Post* wrote, "racists and anti-semites" paraded down Pennsylvania Avenue.

At its height during the 1920s estimates of membership ranged from *three to eight million members.*

The second iteration of the Klan imploded; William Simmons, who had founded the second Klan organization in 1915, was ousted by Hiram Wesley Evans in 1923. It remained active largely in the south. A breakaway group lead by D. C. Stephenson was active in the midwestern states. Stephenson was eventually convicted of abduction, rape and murder of Madge Oberholtzer. His group and the original Simmons-Evans Klan both dropped in membership, to about 30,000 by 1930. and faded away in the 1940s.

The third iteration of the Klan occurred later, in the 1950s and 1960s. During those years the Klan became allied with police departments and governors' offices such as that of George Wallace in Alabama. Klan activities during this third period also included anticommunist efforts.

Several Klan members were convicted of bombing the 16th Street Baptist Church in Birmingham, which caused the deaths of four Black schoolgirls September 15, 1963.

Estimates of current Klan groups are about 30 nationally, members ranging from. 3,000 to 8,000; the FBI and other groups such as the Anti-Defamation League consider the current Klan a terrorist organization. The Southern Poverty Law Center, which tracks such groups, estimates that the number of Klan groups dropped from 130 to just 51 between 2016 -2019.

Into the 1960s and beyond, much of America had become disgusted and repulsed by the beliefs, activities—and violence—of various Klans over the years.

Texan John Howard Griffin served in the South Pacific during World War Two; he lost his eyesight and expected to be blind for the erst of his life. Ten years later, after writing the best-selling book, *The Devil Rides Outside,* while blind, his eyesight suddenly came back and to this day no one knows how or why.

He then decided to experience what it was like to be Black.

He journeyed from his home near Mansfield, Texas to New Orleans and during an intensive week of medications (in a former slave cabin, an irony not lost on him), he did turn his skin a dark, dark black.

Griffin ventured out into the world as a Black man during the pre-Civil Rights years of the late 1950s.

But he *did not know how to be a Black man.*

He spent five weeks as a Black man in the South, terrified that at any moment someone would realize he was actually white. And kill him.

He returned to his home emotionally exhausted but realized that the K1an was active in those years in the Mansfield-Fort

Worth area. If the Klan had found out about his weeks as a Black man in the South, they surely would have come after him, he believed. He took his family to safety in Mexico and lived on property owned by a relative. There he wrote about his experiences and only came back to Texas a year later.

The book he wrote, *Black Like Me,* quickly became—and still is—an American classic. It has been in print now for over 50 years. A 50th year anniversary edition was published in 2011. The Texas Klan never found him.

John Howard Griffin died September 9, 1980; he was 60 years old.

Although he wrote 14 other books throughout his life, *Black Like Me* is his enduring legacy to the world.

The Jim Crow Laws

Few today really understand the origins of "Jim Crow," although they may instinctively know it refers to civil rights and Black deprivations throughout the years.

The actual origins of that term or name came from "Jump Jim Crow," a song-and-dance caricature routine made popular by Thomas D. Rice in 1828; he performed in black face. It became known as a pejorative term for Blacks.

The first use of the term "Jim Crow law" was in *The New York Times* in 1828, referring to an article about segregation in railway cars in Louisiana.

By the end of the 1800s, laws passed in southern states mandating segregation became known as Jim Crow laws. These laws were maintained largely throughout the South from the 1870s into the 1960s.

In fact, these laws institutionalized economic, social class and second-class citizenship for most Blacks living in the South and elsewhere in the United States.

The most famous—or infamous—of these was Plessy v. Ferguson, 1896, in which the U.S. Supreme Court ruled that "separate but equal" educational facilities could be maintained. In actuality, this meant that schools primarily for Black students were ill-equipped in terms of facilities, equipment, supplies and funding.

It took until 1954—58 years—until Brown v. Board of Education (of Topeka, Kansas) made separate but equal illegal. During those 58 years, segregation was solidified and fully enshrined throughout the South. The Brown v. Board of Education decision is now considered a major, major landmark case in civil rights.

Southern states passed laws which made voting difficult or impossible for Blacks. In 1900, there were only 5,320 Black registered voters in Louisiana, although Blacks comprised the majority of citizens of that state at that time. In effect, Blacks were invisible in political systems in the South for decades.

Woodrow Wilson, who was born in the South and who watched *Birth of a Nation* in the White House, the most racist film ever produced, introduced, though his administration, segregation in the federal workplace. His acts were promptly protested by African- American leaders and white civil rights organizations in the North.

Wilson spoke at the Great Reunion of 1913 at Gettysburg, the semi-centennial observance of Lincoln's "All men are created equal speech," also called The Peace Jubilee.

Wilson said:

"How complete the union has become and how dear to all of us, how unquestioned, how benign and majestic, as state after state has been added to this, our great family of free men!"

In rebuttal, historian David W. Blight said the Peace Jubilee at Gettysburg:

" ... was a Jim Crow reunion, and white supremacy might have been said to have been the silent, invisible master of ceremonies."

It took until 1948 for President Harry Truman to integrate the Armed Services of the United States.

In his 1949 book *In the Land of Jim Crow,* Ray Sprigle called the Mason and Dixon line (which unofficially divided the North and the South), "the Smith and Wesson line."

Martin Luther King staged a march in Washington, D.C., in August, 1963, which drew 200,000 in front of the Lincoln Memorial. It was the largest protest in the nation's history. King gave his "I Have a Dream" speech there, which has become one of the most memorable American speeches ever given. The "I Have a Dream" segment was not, as many remember it, at the beginning but much later in his speech.

After John Kennedy was assassinated, President Lyndon Johnson called for the passage of Kennedy's civil rights legislation's program. The United States Senate finally agreed and the Civil Rights Act of 1964 was passed on June 19, 1964. It was the most powerful legislation ever enacted in this area, ever. It guaranteed access to public areas such as restaurants and mandated the Justice Department to sue school systems and other institutions for discrimination. Racial, religious and sexual discriminations were outlawed in business with over 25 employees.

The nation watched in horror as peaceful marchers were attacked by police with billy clubs, mace and dogs as they crossed the Edmund Pettus Bridge in Selma, Alabama, March 7, 1965.

That—and other acts—led to the second major piece of legislation, the Voting Rights Act of 1965, which ended state barriers to voting for all federal, state and local elections, and provided for federal monitoring in counties which had historical records of low minority voter turnout. But that legislation has been challenged in court cases and some of its provisions have been chipped away. In 2013, the Supreme Court under Chief Justice John Roberts, removed the requirement that Southern states needed federal approval for changes in voting policies. Critics of the Supreme Court have warned of other efforts to weaken the Voting Rights Act since that case, officially designated Shelby County v. Holder.

Interracial marriage, made illegal by earlier laws, was rectified by the Earl Warren-led Supreme Court in the case of Loving v. Virginia, made official in 1967.

And yet … and yet … it is common knowledge that Adolf Hitler learned most of his anti-semitism from Henry Ford; Hitler had a picture of Ford in his office (cited earlier).

Did America export any other aspects of hatred to the world?

In a chapter "The Nazis and the Acceleration of Caste" in her 2020 book, *Caste: The Origins of Our Discontents,* Isabel Wilkerson asserts that the German Nazi government got inspiration for its Nuremberg Laws (cited earlier) from the Jim Crow laws in the United States; enacted decades earlier than the Nazi Third Reich.

She writes:

Hitler had studied America from afar, both envying and admiring it, and attributed its achievements to its Aryan stock. He praised the country's near genocide of Native Americas and the exiling to reservations of those who had survived. He was pleased that the United States had "shot down the millions of redskins to a few hundred thousands." He saw the U.S. Immigration Restriction Act of 1924 as a "a model for his program of racial purification, " historian Jonathan Spiro wrote. The Nazis were impressed by the American custom of lynching its subordinate caste of African-Americans, and the exiling to reservations of those who survived." The Nazis were impressed by the American custom of lynching its subordinate caste of African-Americans, having become aware of the ritual torture and mutilations that typically accompanied them.

Hitler especially marveled at the American "knack for maintaining an air of robust innocence in the wake of mass death."

By the time that Hitler rose to power, the United States was not just a country with racism," Whitman, the Yale legal scholar wrote. "It was the leading racial jurisdiction—so much so that even Nazi Germany looked to America for inspiration." The Nazis recognized the parallels even if many Americans did not.

Thus, on the day in June, 1934, as seventeen Reich bureaucrats and legal scholars began to deliberate what would become unprecedented legislation for Germany, they were scrutinizing the United States, and they had done their homework. One of the men, Heinrich Krieger, had studied law in the American South, as an exchange student at the University of Arkansas. He had written extensively about foreign race regimes, having spent two years in South Africa, and was at that very moment completing a book that would be titled *Race Law in the United States* to be published in Germany two years hence. The Nazi lawyers had researched U.S. jurisprudence well enough to know that, from the fugitive slave cases to *Plessy v. Ferguson* and beyond, "the American Supreme Court entertained briefs from Southern States whose arguments were indistinguishable from those of the Nazis," Whitman observed.

Whitman, the Yale scholar that Wilkerson quoted, was James Q. Whitman. She also wrote:

In their search for prototypes, the Nazis had looked into white-dominated countries such Australia and South Africa, but "there were no other models for miscegenation law that the Nazis could find in the world." Whitman wrote. "Their overwhelming interest was in the 'classic example,' the United States of America."

Bobo

In his teenaged years Emmett Till was …

… known as a prankster and risk taker, and a smart dresser who nevertheless did well in school. To his mother (he) was trustworthy, considerate and industrious; and she remembered him as having attended church regularly. Cousins remembered him as the "center of attention," who "liked to be seen. He liked the spotlight."

Another teenager who liked to dress well and liked being in the spotlight was Anne Frank.
Till was also …

… self-assured despite a speech defect—a stutter -- that was a consequence of non-paralytic polio that he had suffered at the age of three. He was about five feet four or five inches tall, weighted about 160 pounds and was muscular and stocky.

His mother once said (to coin a cliché), "if every problem was a lock, Emmett had a ring of keys."
He was born outside Chicago July 25, 1941.
His family nickname was Bobo.

The Encounter at the Store

In *A Death in the Delta: The Story of Emmett Till*, Stephen J. Whitfield writes:

> Two cents' worth of bubble gum and a girl's picture in a wallet—these were the paltry artifacts of ordinary life, the commonplace detritus that decorated the genesis of the case. But however unspectacular the *mise-en-scene*, this was one murder that has remained entrenched in memory, and the interest and publicity that it galvanized may, finally, be among its most salient features.

And, he writes:

> Till was murdered in an era when it was no longer politically prudent for the lives of people of color to be extinguished so brutally. For in James Baldwin's lapidary words, "this world is white no longer and it will never be white again." Indeed, in that sense not even the south was ever to be white again—for political power would cease to be exclusively color-coded, and that became the condition of the Delta as well.

Decades before, in the early twentieth century, Mark Twain was calling his native land "The United States of Lyncherdom."

In her massive 620-page cultural history. *The Warmth of Other Suns: The Epic Story of America's Great Migration*, Isabel Wilkerson writes:

> They left as if under a spell or a high fever. "They left as though they were fleeing some curse," wrote the scholar Emmett J. Scott. "They were willing to make almost any sacrifice to obtain a railroad ticket, and they left with the intention of staying."
>
> From the early years of the twentieth century to well past its middle age, nearly every black family in the American South, which meant nearly every black family in America, had a decision to make. There were share-croppers losing at settlement. Typists wanting to work in an office. Yard boys scared that a single gesture near the planter's wife could leave them hanging from an oak tree. They were all stuck in a caste system as hard and unyield-ing as the red Georgia clay, and they each had a decision before them. In this, they were not unlike anyone who-ever longed to cross the Atlantic or the Rio Grande.
>
> It was during the First World War that a silent pil-grimage took its first steps within the borders of this country. The fever rose without warning or notice or much in the way of understanding by those outside its reach. It would not end until the 1970s and would set in motion changes in the North and South that no one, not even the people doing the leaving, could have imagined at the start or dreamed would take nearly a lifetime to play out.
>
> Historians would came to call it the Great Migration. It would become perhaps the biggest underreported story of the twentieth century. It was vast. It was leaderless. It

crept along so many thousands of currents over such a long stretch of time as to be difficult for the press truly to capture while it was underway.

Over the course of six decades, some six million black southerners left the land of their forefathers and fanned out across the country for an uncertain existence in nearly every other corner of America. The Great Migration would become a turning point in history. It transformed urban America and recast the social and political order of every city it touched.

It would force the South to search its soul and finally to lay aside a feudal caste system. It grew out of the unmet promises made after the Civil War and, through the sheer weight of it, helped push the country toward the civil rights revolution of the 1960s.

Mamie Till-Mobley's family—the Carthans—were part of the hordes who left the rural south for better lives in the urban north, as described in Isabel Wilkerson's epic analysis, *The Warmth of Other Suns.*

In *Death of Innocence: The Story of the Hate Crime That Changed America,* Mamie Till-Mobley writes that perhaps as many as two hundred thousand Blacks left the south for the Chicago area in the 1920s and 1930s. Most, she said, were from Mississippi.

Her family members got work at the Corn Products company, which made syrup and other corn-related products in Argo, Illinois, outside Chicago.

She writes:

We had come to Argo from outside Webb, Mississippi, where I was born, near Sumner. My daddy, Wiley Nash Carthan, had come up a couple months ahead of us and found work at Corn Products. Mama and I joined him in January, 1924, when I was a little over two years old. As far as Mama was concerned, we didn't come a moment too soon. All kinds of stories came out of Mississippi with the black people who were running for their lives. There had been talk of a lynching in Greenwood, Mississippi. It was the sort of horrible thing you only hear of in the areas nearby. But it seemed like that was the whole point: to send a signal, to make sure that black people in the area were kept under control. Maybe it was that Mama just knew she could never be controlled, or maybe she just knew there had to be a better life for us somewhere else. And just about any place would have been better than Mississippi in the 1920s.

There were so many Blacks coming to that area they called it "little Mississippi."

Mamie Carthan met and eventually married Louis Till. Their only child, Emmett, was born July 25, 1941 in Cook County Hospital in Chicago. In 1955, when Emmett was 14, he decided that he was old enough to travel by himself by train to Money, Mississippi to visit his uncle Moses Wright and various distant relatives. His mother Mamie knew full well what Money, Mississippi, was like. As she wrote in her memoir, *Death of Innocence:*

Somewhere around seven in the evening on Wednesday, August 24, after supper when papa Mose was in church, Maurice, Wheeler, Bo (Bobo), Simeon, Roosevelt Crawford, and Roosevelt's niece, Ruthie Crawford climbed into Papa Mose's car and drove uptown. Although there were as couple of hundred people who lived around Money, the town itself was little more than one street. Not a street, really. It was more like what somebody once called "a wide place in the road." A whistle-stop. It was a lazy place. Easy to feel relaxed there. In Money, there were no obvious signs of trouble. None of the things Emmett had been warned about. No "White" or "Colored" drinking fountains, no segregated sections on buses, nobody stepping off sidewalks to let white folks pass. But that was because there were no drinking fountains, there were no buses, there were no sidewalks. Money wasn't like other places in the Jim Crow south. It was worse. It was much worse. The dangers were hidden, and a lot more treacherous. It was a place with racial attitudes as rigid as an oak tree in the dead of winter. People who lived in the area knew where the lines were, knew not to cross them. They didn't need signs to direct them. They didn't need help abiding by the rules, just like they didn't need help breathing. It was in them. A basic life function. For outsiders, things weren't that obvious.

It was the most improbable plane, yet the most likely place, for a racial incident that would set off nation-wide repercussions. And change the country forever.

They all drove to Bryant's Grocery and Meat Market. Owned by Roy Bryant, who was out of town, the store catered to Black residents of the area who could buy small items there and play checkers outside. His wife, Carolyn Bryant, was the only clerk in the store.

Other youngsters in the party went in and out. Then Emmett went inside.

He and Carolyn Bryant were the two key people in the store.

Time has blurred what happened. In fact, Carolyn Bryant changed her story from time to time in the years after the incident. She admitted she lied about the incident during the trial of her husband and his half-brother, J. W. "Big" Milam, making it sound worse than it was. Timothy Tyson, author of *The Blood of Emmett Till,* later said she "was the mouthpiece of a monstrous lie."

In the years and decades since, she told and re-told versions of the encounter story in different variations that she may not, in her later years, have known the truth of what actually happened.

Did Emmett Till ask her for a date? Did he tell her, or just imply, he was from the North? Did he brag that he "had been with white women before"? During those years men's wallets were sold with movie star photos inside. He showed her his wallet with a photo. It might have been actress Hedy Lamarr. Did he imply that she was his girlfriend? Did he grab Carolyn Bryant by the arm at one point, across the counter?

None of this would have been in any way consequential in any store in the North. A white female store clerk in Argo, Illinois, would have laughed off the whole encounter or at worst, told him to leave.

None of this was standard behavior expected of Black men in Money, Mississippi. Not an ounce of it.

What were her emotions in those moments? Was she outraged? Frightened? Terrified by this young Black boy from the North? Was she apprehensive? Fearful? Was she on an adrenaline high alone at that point? No one will ever know.

But she did run outside to a car to get a gun. She later said she thought she would be raped.

And then—even worse—others outside heard a whistle.

Later some said it was a wolf whistle; a leering sexual come-on.

Did Emmett Till whistle at her?

(He did have a speech imperfection, from a bout of non-paralytic polio when he was a preschooler. He was taught by his mother that if he was having trouble pronouncing some words he should speak slowly, but that produced a slight whistle.)

A Black man, no matter what age, whistling at, or leering at, a white woman would have meant an automatic death sentence in Money, Mississippi and, in fact, elsewhere in the south during those times.

Some onlookers claimed—or believed—he was whistling at those playing checkers outside the store.

She did, however say, in a 2008 interview, "Nothing that boy did would ever justify what happened to him."

Too little, too late.

Far, far, far too late. Decades too late.

Carolyn Bryant later wrote a memoir, *I Am More Than a Wolf Whistle*, with the stipulation it could not be published until after her death. She died April 25, 2023, in Westlake, Louisiana. She was 88.

The store in Money, Mississippi, was featured in *The New York Times* article "Emmett Till's murder and How American Remembers Its Darkest Moments," by Audra S. Burch, Veda Shastri and Tim Chafee, published February 20, 2019. A video clip from above (taken by a drone?) scans the building; it a complete ruin, with the roof completely gone, shrubbery and such growing inside the building. There have been some thoughts of rebuilding the grocery as a civil rights monument, but no consensus has been formed. It is a ruin; it justifiably should stay that way.

Roy Bryant, one of the two men who kidnapped and, lynched Emmett Till came from a family that was described, more than once as "poor white trash." His mother began each day with bourbon and drank throughout the day. Carolyn Bryant once said "They were racist, the whole family. For one thing it was the 'N-word' all the time. 'I've got this N working for me over here doing this, I'm gonna have to go get my money from that N over there because he's not paying me.'"

Roy and his half brother, J.W. "Big" Milam both carried guns.

Both had been in the service during World War Two. Bryant enlisted at 18; Milam got thorough the tenth grade before going the Army; Milam served in the 2nd Armored Division from 1941 through 1946, even earning a battlefield promotion to lieutenant, a Silver Star, a Purple Heart and other medals.

In his book *The Blood of Emmett Till*, Timothy Tyson has this segment about J.W. Milam. The "Huie" in this segment is William Bradford Huie, who later used "checkbook journalism"—paying Byrant and Milam for their stories—for an article subsequently published in *Look* magazine. Checkbook journalism was unethical during Huie's time and is unethical now. Journalists simply don't pay interview subjects for their stories, but Huie thought it the only way to get Bryant and Milam to tell their side of the Till lynching, as horrific as it was. (The cost was $4,000; $1,000 to their attorney and the rest divided between them.)

J. J. Breland, a local attorney, regarded J.W. (Milam) as a kind of brutal necessity for the social order of white supremacy. "He comes from a big, mean, overbearing family," Breland said bluntly. "Got a chip on his shoulder. That's how he got that battlefield promotion in Europe: he likes to kill folks. But, hell, we'e got to have our Milams to fight our wars and keep the niggahs in line." One of four lawyers who would defend Milam and Bryant, Breland told Huie to let the country know that integration was out of the question in Mississippi. "The whites own all the property in Tallahatchie County. We don't need the niggers no more." Of course this was hardly the case for the Bryants and Milams, who relied almost entirely on African Americans for their livelihood. Nor would they likely have agreed with Breland, despite their relative poverty, about their social position among white Mississippians.

Milam was, essentially, a racist enforcer in Mississippi, even more so than Bryant.

The Byrants and Milams were only one-half step above the *niggahs* they despised, but whom they needed—sometimes desperately needed—for their own meager living.

In addition to *poor white trash,* another common expression which described the Bryants and Milams was *peckerwoods;* on the lowest rung of white society there, or perhaps under the lowest rung of the white society ladder.

Roy Bryant was off carting shrimp to Texas in a truck when his wife encountered Emmett Till; when he returned, she told him of her encounter. Her story was doubtlessly inaccurate, perhaps lurid. She said she thought she would be raped during that encounter.

Bryant and Big Milam went to find Moses Wright; he would have the boy with him or know where he was.

They barged into Wright's sharecropper's cabin at 2 a.m, with flashlights and pistols. The boy was there. They told him to get dressed.

They asked Wright, "How old are you?'

"Sixty-four," he said.

"If you say anything to anyone about this, you'll never reach sixty-five."

They took the boy with them into the Mississippi night. That was the last time anyone saw Emmett Till alive.

The Funeral

Less than three days after Emmett Till was taken away, a 17-year old sharecropper's son saw a body in the Tallahatchie river. Even Carolyn Bryant was surprised; she had been told that her husband and Big Milam had kidnapped the boy, but let him go. (Later during the Bryant-Milam trial, defense lawyers tried to claim the boy had been found by the NAACP and they had quickly sent him to Chicago or Detroit or—*who knows where?* He could be anywhere in the North by now, they said.)

The site where the body was found was only about 15 miles from where Till's mother Mamie was born.

Sheriffs deputies had a hard time pulling the body from the river; an iron fan, almost one hundred pounds, used to ventilate cotton gins, was lashed to the body's neck with several feet of barbed wire, presumably making the body so heavy it would never surface.

After the discovery of the body became known, one white local said, "that river's lull of niggers."

Chester Miller, a black undertaker working for the Century Burial Association, was called in to help retrieve the body. Timothy Tyson quotes in him in *The Blood of Emmett Till:*

The crown of his head was just crushed out and in, and a piece of his skull fell out there in the boat, maybe three inches long (and) maybe two and one half inches wide, something like that.

There was a hole perhaps half an inch square above the right ear, which Miller assumed was a bullet hole. Later it was discovered the hole went completely through the skull. One eyeball had fallen out of place. The other eye was simply gone.

Analysis: Emmett Till was severely beaten then shot in the head.

Initially it was thought the body could not be identified; the body had been in the river so long and had decomposed so badly it was almost impossible to tell if the person was white or Black.

Undertakers in Mississippi and later in Chicago tried to do some touch-up work on the face and head, but little could be done.

But there was one key item which identified the body.

Mamie Till's husband Louis had been in trouble. Trouble here, trouble there. Finally a judge gave him a choice: go to jail or join the Army. Till joined the Army and served in Italy from 1940 to 1945.

Then Mamie Till got a document from the Army with the term "Willful Misconduct." She had no idea what that meant; neither did anyone else. She soon found out; in Italy, Louis Till had raped two Italian women and killed a third. He was executed by the Army for that "Willful Misconduct." General Dwight Eisenhower signed the Army documents. Because of that reason, there were no death benefits for the family. A few personal items were returned. One item was a silver ring with the initials LT: Louis Till. Emmett Till wore his father's silver ring.

The ring was found on the body in the Tallahatchie River.

Soon after, an arrest warrant was issued for Carolyn Bryant's part in the whole affair, for kidnapping. A legitimate arrest warrant, but it was never served. The document was discovered only years later.

Why? Why was it never served?

"She had two children and we didn't want to bother her," white officials said.

> A legitimate arrest warrant. Never served.
> "We didn't want to bother her."
> Southern justice in Mississippi in 1955.
> Southern **white** justice in Mississippi in 1955.

White officials in Mississippi wanted to bury the body as soon as possible without ceremony and thus bury the entire incident—to conceal and bury the whole story. But Mamie Till refused. Refused to let her son be buried in Mississippi. She consulted the most widely known black funeral director in the Chicago area. Bringing the body back by train would cost $3,300, back then. Do it, she said, I'll get the money.

She then insisted on an open casket funeral, so the world could see "what they did to my boy." The casket had a glass top that sealed in an horrific odor.

Newspapers including *The Chicago Tribune* reported that "More than 40,000 persons viewed the body in the afternoon and into the night" on the first day of viewing at the A.A. Rayner and Sons funeral home. Lines ran around the block and beyond. The funeral home had to set up a special rest-and-recovery area, for viewers overcome by the sight of Till's body. Ushers were alerted to catch those ready to faint. (The U.S. Holocaust Museum in Washington D.C., has a similar rest- and-recovery area, for visitors overcome by the enormity of the six-story self-guided tour of the Holocaust.)

Photographers took pictures of Till in the casket; they were run in *Ebony* and *Jet,* two Black magazines owned by the same company. Both had national circulations.

One photographer, Ernest Withers, took a close-up of Till's mutilated face. That photograph ran nationally in in *Jet* magazine four days before the Bryant-Milam trial.

The Tribune subsequently reported, "Capt. Albert Anderson, in charge of a large police detail at the (Roberts Temple Church of God in Christ) church said that more than 100,000 persons had viewed the remains of the youth."

The Chicago Defender, a newspaper for Black readers estimated the number at 250,000 viewers. "All were shocked, some horrified, some appalled. Many prayed, scores fainted, and practically all, men, women and children, wept."

The prevalent emotions seemed to be anguish and outrage, in equal measure.

Television stations in Chicago covered the events extensively and fed their stories to the national networks, making it a "media circus," and resulted in msgor coverage of the upcoming Mississippi trial of Bryant and Milam.

Mamie Till's insistence that the remains of her son—her beloved baby Bobo—be brought back north and her insistence of an open casket funeral sparked a revolution. It began the Civil Rights years which continue to this day. There have been murders since: Medger Evers killed in Mississippi and and the Rev. Martin Luther King Jr., killed in Memphis are but two notable examples, but the crusade for justice and civil rights continues. And the brutal lynching in Mississippi, of a young Black boy from the Chicago area, was the tipping point.

The Trial

The trial of Roy Bryant and Big Milam became the biggest media circus since the Lindbergh baby kidnapping trial, which began in Flemington, New Jersey, the first week of January, 1935. Bruno Richard Hauptmann was eventually convicted of kidnapping and killing the son of aviator Charles Lindbergh.

The Bryant-Milam trial was held in the small town of Sumner, Mississippi, in Tallahatchie County, which had never seen such an event before. The kidnapping had taken place in Leflore county, to the south, but the body had been found in the Tallahatchie River, in Tallahatchie County, north of Money, Mississippi.

The newly-elected sheriff of Tallahatchie county was Henry Clarence Strider, known as H.C. In *The Blood of Emmett Till*, Timothy Tyson describes him as

... a 270 pound former football player who owned 1,500 acres of prime Delta cotton land and held sway over dozens of sharecropping families. Carolyn (Bryant) described him as "sort of like the Godfather in Mississippi at the time.

"Whatever he said is what you did."

And Tyson writes,

... the Milams and Bryants enjoyed his protection from the law and from everyone else. "One reason they were so much the way they were was that they though they were right with him." Through Strider would prove to be a lordly ally, his vassals remained penniless peckerwoods.

In short, he was Big Milam with a badge. And more money.

When the trial began the courthouse was packed with reporters from all over the outside world. Timothy Tyson wrote there was 100 journalists and 30 photographers attending from: New York; Chicago; Memphis; Detroit; Miami; Atlanta; New Orleans; Pittsburgh; Toledo; Washington; London and elsewhere.

Publications included: *Time; Newsweek; Life, The Nation.*

They included representatives from: *The Memphis Press-Scimitar; The Jackson Daily* News; the National Negro Press Association; *Ebony* and *Jet* magazines; *The Chicago Defender,* and others. White writers such as Murray Kampton and David Halberstam wrote about the Till case. Halberstam's reportage later appeared as a 10-page section in his massive (733 page) book *The Fifties,* first published in 1993.

Western Union set up a special wire service on the court-house lawn, so articles could be sent out to newspapers quickly.

Newspapers in Jakarta; Copenhagen; Dusseldorf; Paris; Istanbul; Rome and Stockholm were interested in the Till drama.

The atmosphere appeared to be "controlled hostility."

White Mississippians were outraged that northern writers were questioning their way of life which had worked for them for decades.

Northerners were equally outraged at the racism that simmered and boiled just barely below the surface in Mississippi.

Sheriff Strider and others were warned—or perhaps it was suggested—that they all should be on their best behavior for the world to see.

Strider walked through the courtroom, with a cheerful "good morning niggers ..."

And although Strider was the Sheriff and presumably an officer of the court and presumably should remain neutral, he testified *for the defense* during the trial.

Even in the courtroom, seating was highly segregated.

During the trial, Representative Charles C. Diggs, of Michigan sent word to the judge, Charles Swango, that he wanted to attend the trial, presumably not only to witness the court proceedings, but to also perhaps help ease the segregation situation. Diggs was one of only three Black members of the 84th U.S. Congress.

Diggs appeared and gave his card to James Hicks, a reporter for *The Amsterdam News* and the National Negro Press Association, to give to court deputies.

That led to this incident, which Stephen J. Whitfield reported in *A Death in the Delta:*

> By the time the representative got inside the courtroom, the whites and blacks had already taken all the seats. Diggs gave his card to Hicks, who started up to the judge's bench, but was accosted by a deputy who inquired: "Where are you going nigger?" When Hicks explained his mission, and showed the deputy the card, another deputy was called over and was told: "This nigger said there's another nigger outside who says he's a Congressman ..."

"A nigger Congressman?"

"That's what this nigger said," then the first deputy laughed at such a blatant contradiction in terms. But the sheriff was summoned and then told Hicks: "I'll bring him in here, but I'm going to sit him at you niggers' table." And that's where the representative sat.

There were seven attorneys in the immediate area, all white males. All volunteered to work for the defense and work *pro bono.*

The jury was all white. All white men. No white women. No Blacks. Nine white cotton farmers, two carpenters and an insurance salesman were selected.

In Mississippi a prospective jury member had to be a registered voter. Intimidation and threats kept Blacks from voting: *"Nigger, how old are you? If you want to live past your next birthday, don't think of trying to vote. Understand me?"*

A common phrase, known throughout Mississippi was: *if you're tired of living, vote and die.*

Bryant and Milam were both indicted for murder. Carolyn Bryant indicted for kidnapping.

The prosecution case was strong. Byrant and Milam had admitted kidnapping Till; that was clear. The prosecution called Moses Wright to the witness stand. (Blacks were invariably called by their first names. The Defense always said Mose, or Uncle Mose, when he was on the witness stand.) He had watched the two men kidnap Till from his home. Asked if he knew the defendants, he slowly rose from the witness chair and pointed to Byrant and Milam, knowing he might easily be killed later on any given dark Mississippi night. Or even in broad daylight.

After the trial, he kept a loaded shotgun bedside his bed, but very soon gave away his favorite hunting dog, abandoned his car at the nearest train station and left the state, Stephen J. Whitfield writes.

The defense claimed that although they had kidnapped Till, they had let him go. The NAACP was actually the culprit here, the Defense claimed. They spirited the boy away to the north and he was alive in Chicago or Detroit or … who knows where.

Mamie Till journeyed back into Mississippi and appeared as a witness. She was calm and steadfast, and identified, from a picture, that the body in the river and subsequently sent to Chicago, was her son. The jury foreman was asked later about her testimony: "If she tried a little harder, she might have gotten out a tear."

The Defense claimed the body in the Tallahatchie River was so decomposed there was no way to identify it, white or Black. (The silver ring with the initials LT ?—well, someone could have it put it there on the body … sometime.)

The jury deliberated (if you could call it that) for an hour.

The verdict: Not Guilty.

Jury members later said they were told they should take a period of time to make the verdict deliberations seem reasonable. They later said that the verdict could have been announced earlier than an hour, but they were all drinking Cokes in the jury room. (Cokes *and beer* were apparently sold *in the courtroom* during the trial, without complaint from the judge.)

Emotions at Emmett Till's open casket funeral in the Chicago area were mixed: anguish and outrage, in equal portions.

Reactions to the verdict were simply—in most cases outside Mississippi, and elsewhere in the Old South—outrage.

The Christian Century; The Pittsburgh Courier (a Black newspaper), *Commonweal,* and a wide variety of other newspapers and magazines expressed the same.

The news skyrocketed around the world: *Le Figaro,* in Paris condemned the verdict, as did as the weekly newspaper *France*

Observateur. Even in the Vatican, the official publication, the *L'Osservatore Romano,* also condemned the verdict.

In Dusseldorf, *Das Freie Volk (The Free People)* stated that "the life of a Negro in Mississippi is not worth a whistle."

Enter William Bradford Huie; he was a journalist, a native of Alabama and graduate of the University of Alabama. After the verdict, Bryant and Milam were aware that they could not be tried for murder again, under the commonly accepted legal rules of Double Jeopardy.

They then freely announced that, yes, they had murdered Emmett Till.

Huie claimed he was an equal of Milam—Huie said he could drink (moonshine?) "from the same jug with Milam and give Milam the first swig." He negotiated with Bryant and Milam to tell their stories. "Checkbook journalism": he paid them for their admissions / confessions. $4,000. Their lawyer got $1,000. The rest was split between the two. In turn, they agreed that they couldn't sue Huie later for libel.

Huie apparently didn't ask the questions; their attorney did.

Huie believed this was the only way he could get Bryant and Milam to tell their stories—pay them. This is the most famous— or infamous case—of "Checkbook Journalism" in American journalism history

Bryant and Milam had taken Till in the back of a green pickup truck toward Drew, Mississippi, then drove to a small barn, or shed, where they beat him savagely. Willie Reed, a black teenager, 18 at the time, heard sounds of the beating from outside the shed. He was later approached by Milam who asked if he had heard anything. He prudently said, no he hadn't and Milam let him go. Others saw blood in the back of the pickup truck and a boot. Milam said he had shot a deer (which presumably explained the blood) and the boot was his.

Huie's article, "The Shocking Story of Approved Killing in Mississippi" was published in *Look* magazine, January 1956. In the article, Huie quotes Big Milam:

"Well, what else could we do? He was hopeless. I'm no bully. I never hurt a nigger in my life. I like niggers— in their place— I know how to work 'em. But I just decided it was time a few people got put on notice. As long as I live and can do something about it, niggers are gonna stay in their place. Niggers ain't gonna vote where I live. If they did, they'd control the government. They ain't gonna go to school with my kids. And when a nigger gets close to mentioning sex with a white woman, he's tired of livin'. I'd likely kill him. Me and my folks fought for this country and we got some rights. I stood there in that shed and listened to that nigger throw that poison at me, and just made up my mind. 'Chicago boy.' I said, 'I'm, tired of 'em sending your kin down here to stir up trouble. Goddam you, I'm going to make an example of you— just so everybody can know how me and my folks stand.'"

Outside the Deep South: Three Reasons Why National Racial Justice Was Slow

In *Death in the Delta*, Stephen J. Whitfield follows the Till case into the thickets of Washington, D.G., during the Eisenhower administration. He writes:

> The shock of the Till murder even reverberated to the inner sanctum of the Executive branch in Washington, and that sort of federal attention was unprecedented for a Southern crime of racial violence. It was nevertheless a "misfortune for blacks in America," the historian William E. Leuchtenberg has observed, "that in the year the Supreme Court handed down the Brown decision Dwight Eisenhower was president of the United states." Despite the publicity provided by the trial in Sumner, the federal government showed itself to be quite indifferent to the "jungle fury" that the NAACP charged was prevailing in the state of Mississippi.

> The president himself was hostile to black aspiration for first-class citizenship. He had opposed the

desegregation for the armed forces and well as the establishment of the Fair Employment Practices Commission in the 1940s. Nor did Eisenhower see the necessity for the enforcement or passage of laws designed to protect the civil rights of blacks in the south or elsewhere. Unlike Faulkner, the president failed to speak out against white racist violence—a problem that he evaded so fully that reporters discovered his ignorance that such incidents had even occurred.

And, Whitfield wrote:

Indeed, he told Chief Justice Earl Warren that the segregationists were "not bad people. All they were concerned about is to see that their sweet little girls aren't required to sit in schools alongside some big overgrown Negroes."

That prompted Roy Wilkins, of the NAACP, to reply: "Eisenhower was a fine general and a good decent man; but if he had fought World War II the way he fought for civil rights we would all be speaking German today"

Additionally, in his essay "Why don't we remember Ike as a civil rights leader?" in 2014, Adam Serwer writes:

In two terms as president, Eisenhower combined what was, at the time, the strongest record on civil rights since Reconstruction with a baffling rhetorical deference to white supremacists and a cold relationship with civil rights leaders.

Eisenhower opposed discrimination but seems to sympathize far more with the white Southerners whose lives would be disrupted by the end of Jim Crow than blacks dwelling under its boot heel. He was an incrementalist skeptical of federal power who often repeated the ideological belief that laws could not shape culture, despite pursuing laws that would extend— albeit modestly compared to Johnson-era efforts—federal authority to protect Americans' civil rights. Eisenhower would say, "you cannot change peoples' hearts merely by laws."

And, secondly then, the intransigence of Southern U.S. Senators, Southern Governors, George Wallace, Orval Faubus and others, down to Bull Connor, and Southern U.S Congressmen who never wanted *any* racial reforms—then—and many others still do not, to this day.

Finally, J. Edgar Hoover was acknowledged to be a racist then, and acknowledged to be so today. He refused to get the FBI involved, believing no federal laws had been broken and thus the FBI had no jurisdiction in the case. Whitfield charges that Hoover did not have imagination enough to establish a reason for the FBI to be involved. White racist crimes in the South were not given high priority in Hoover's FBI or in federal offices in Washington, D.C.

Hoover was more comfortable in blaming the American version of the Communist Party. The Communist Party, USA, was then an easy target. Hoover, at one time, implied, or stated, that Mamie Till was a "tool of the Communist party."

Nonetheless, the FBI did compile a file on the Till case, *pro forma* and relatively inconsequential.

Later, J. Edgar Hoover called Dr. Martin Luther King Jr., "The most notorious liar in the United States," and carried on a years-long personal vendetta against King, which ultimately included a huge FBI file, which may be released in 2027.

Denouements
The legacies of
Emmett Till
Carolyn Byrant
Roy Bryant and J.W. "Big" Milam

Emmett Till

In 1976, a statue was unveiled in Denver with. Martin Luther King Jr. holding an arm on Emmett Till's shoulders. It has since been moved to Pueblo, Colorado.

In 1984, a section of 71st Street in Chicago was named "Emmett Till Road" and in 2005, the 71st Street Bridge was also named for Till.

In 1989, Till was among 40 names who died in the Civil Rights movement, listed on a granite sculpture on the Civil Rights Memorial in Montgomery, Alabama. They are all named as martyrs.

Till was named in 2000 as part of the celebration of the 36th anniversary of the crossing of the Edmund Pettus Bridge, in Selma, Alabama. A demonstration was held in his honor and Mamie Till attended.

In 2004, James McCosh Elementary School, where Till attended, was renamed the "Emmett Louis Till Math and Science Academy."

In 2006, the "Emmett Till Memorial Highway" was dedicated between Greenwood and Tutwiler, Mississippi. This was the route his body was taken to the nearest train station, to be returned to Chicago.

In 2006, the Emmett Till Memorial Commission was established by the Tallahatchie Board of Supervisors.

In 2007, that Commission issued a formal apology to Till's family:

> We the citizens of Tallahatchie County recognize that the Emmett Till case was a terrible miscarriage of justice.
>
> We state candidly and with deep regret the failure to effectively pursue justice. We wish to say to the family of Emmett Till that we are profoundly sorry for what was done in this community to your loved one.

Also in 2007, Congressman John Lewis of Georgia sponsored a bill to provide a plan for investigating and prosecuting unsolved (cold cases) Civil Rights-era murders. The Emmett Till Unsolved Civil Rights Crime Act was signed into law in 2008.

In 2008, a sign *was* erected near the Tallahatchie River where Till's body was found. It was pulled up and apparently thrown into the river by vandals. A second sign was erected and subsequently riddled with bullet holes. A third sign was set up and it too, was riddled by bullets. A fourth sign is now up, said to be bullet-proof.

The Tallahatchie County Courthouse where the Bryant-Milam trial was held was refurbished and re-opened in 2012, but across the street is now the Emmett Till Interpretive Center.

The Emmett Till Memorial Project is a website associated with the Interpretative Center, that shows 51 sites in the Mississippi Delta related to the Till story.

In 2015, Florida State University opened the Emmett Till Archives.

In 2020, the National Trust for Historic Preservation named the Roberts Temple Church of God in Christ, where Till's funeral was held, as one of America's most endangered historic sites.

And in 2022, the United States Congress awarded Emmett Till and his mother Mamie the Congressional Gold Medal.

Shortly thereafter, Congress also passed the Emmett Till Antilynching Act—*67 years*—after Emmett Till was lynched in Mississippi.

A sign was placed on a Mississippi road near where
Emmett Till's body was thrown into the Tallahatchie River.
The sign was torn up and thrown into the river.
The second and third signs were riddled with gunshots.
A fourth sign is said to be bullet-proof.

Carolyn Bryant

Carolyn Bryant, the woman Emmett Till met in the store in Money, Mississippi, an encounter which led to his gruesome death, died April 25, 2023, in Louisiana. She was 88. Her death was reported nationally and major obituaries appeared in *The New York Times*, *The Washington Post* and elsewhere.

She divorced Roy Byrant, moved, remarried and for the rest of her days, become elusive, hiding from her role in the Till lynching.

She told and retold the encounter story over the years, that essentially, she could not remember, or later did not know, the true story of that day.

She did, however, say, in 2008, "Nothing that boy did could ever justify what happened to him."

Her legacy remains, charitably, mixed at best.

Roy Bryant and J. W. "Big" Milam

With their hardscrabble lives and inadequate educations neither Roy Bryant nor Big Milam would have known the word *pariah*; with the Not Guilty court decision, they might have hoped to become heroes—saviors in the Deep South, defending White Southern Womanhood.

But without knowing that word, they quickly did become pariahs in their native state. Even in the sweltering racism of Mississippi, Bryant and Milam had gone too far:

- In the first three weeks after the Sumner Not Guilty verdict, Bryant's store in Money, Mississippi, did not clear one hundred dollars. The local Blacks that Bryant depended on as customers, simply disappeared.
- When he returned to Sumner to withdraw savings from a local bank, he was told to never return to Sumner again.
- Other residents of Mississippi didn't want them as neighbors, thinking logically: "if those two did that to a boy—even a Black boy—they would do the same to my (white) family."
- Bryant had to depend on part-time jobs, some for as little as 75 cents a day.
- *He and his family eventually moved out of Mississippi into East Texas. He had learned—on the G.I. Bill—to be a welder and spent 15 years as a boilermaker, but that trade cost him much of his eyesight. When he died he was legally blind.
- He eventually returned to Mississippi to again run a small store, but was twice found guilty of federal food

stamp fraud. Bryant's wife divorced him; Milam's wife divorced him.

- Milam continued to work as a farmer, but he was too poor to buy land and was usually unable to rent land either. Mississippi banks refused to give him crop loans. When he did have some crops to harvest, black sharecroppers refused to work for him; white sharecroppers insisted on more than he had been paying for Black help.
- Milam had moved to East Texas to be with Bryant, but he too, returned to Mississippi.
- Unable to do much else he became a bootlegger. He was arrested at least once for bootlegging.
- Both remained pariahs for the rest of their lives.
- Milam died of spinal cancer Dec. 31, 1981. (Bryant died later.) Bryant subsequently said this about Milam (emphasis added):

"He *was a hell of a fine fellow and brother. He was as gentle as a lamb and helped a lot of people.*"

Gentle as a lamb. Until he killed Emmett Till.

Both were virulent unrepentant racists and self-confessed killers.

Annotated Bibliography

Anne Frank House. *Anne Frank In the World, 1929-1945.*
   New York: Scholastic, 2000.
   Largely a picture book, for schools.

Arendt, Hannah. *Eichmann, in Jerusalem:*
   A Study in the Banality of Evil.
   New York: The Viking Press, 1965.
   Her best-selling book, but marred by major errors in: com-
   position / writing style; largely incorrect assumptions about
   Eichmann and reportage techniques. (She only briefly attended
   the lengthy trial and depended almost completely on court
   transcripts. Her book appears to show she witnessed Eichmann's
   execution, which was not true. See the chapter on Arendt in
   The Books That Haunt Us.)

Barnouw, David and Gerrold Van Der Strom, Eds.
   The Dairy of Anne Frank: The Critical Edition.
   New York: Doubleday, 1989.
   Contains every diary entry by Anne Frank and indicates if the
   version was her first (Version A) or her revisions (Version B) or
   other revisions by her Father after World War Two (Version C).
   Massive—700 pages—including sections about the arrest of
   those in the Secret Annex; the Betrayal, Imprisonment, the play
   based on her Diary and attacks on the authenticity of the diary.
   A caveat: the type is very, very small; readers might be advised

to use the 1995 Definitive Edition. This version prepared by the Netherlands State Institute for War Documentation. Pricey on the internet and relatively rare.

Bartlett, Karen. *The Dairy That Changed the World: The Remarkable Story of Otto Frank and the Diary of Anne Frank.* London: Biteback Publishing, 2022.

Birth of a Nation. 1915. D.W. Griffith. Starring Lillian Gish. DVD available from Amazon, e-Bay and other sources.

Bloom, Harold, Ed., *A Scholarly Look at The Dairy of Anne Frank.*
Philadelphia, Pa.: Chelsea House Publishers, 1999.

Burch, Audra, Vida Shastri and Tim Chafee. "Emmett Till's Murder and How America Remembers Its Darkest Moments."
The New York Times, Feb. 20, 2019.
This New York Times article has a short videoclip from above (taken by a drone?) showing how the county store is now in ruins, where Emmett Till encountered Carolyn Bryant.

Cole. Tim. *Selling the Holocaust.*
From Auschwitz to Schindler:
How History is Bought, Packaged and Sold.
New York: Rout-ledge, 2000.
Contains major sections on Anne Frank, Adolf Eichmann and Oscar Schindler.

Fensch, Thomas, *at the dangerous edge of social justice: race, violence and death in America.*
N. Chesterfield, Va.: New Century Books, 2013.

_____. *The Books That Haunt Us.*
N. Chesterfield Va., News Century Books, 2020.
Contains major analyses of (in order of publication):
Hiroshima, *Hersey;* If This is a Man, *Levi;* Night, *Weisel;*
Eichmann in Jerusalem, *Arendt and other, non–World War*
Two titles.

_____. *The Man Who Changed His Skin:*
The Life and Work of John Howard Griffin.
N. Chesterfield, Va.: New Century Books, 2011.
The only full biography of Griffin, who dyed his skin black and
toured the south in the pre–Civil Rights era. Fearing the Klu
Klux Klan, which was active in his native Texas in the late
1950s, he lived in Mexico for a year while writing Black Like
Me, *which quickly became—and still is—an American classic.*

_____. *Oscar Schindler and His List:*
The Man, the Book, the Film, the Holocaust and Its Survivors.
Middlebury, Vt.,: Paul S. Eriksson, Publisher, 1995.
Contains an Annotated Bibliography of 137 Holocaust titles.

_____. *The Sordid Hypocrisy of To Protest and to Serve:*
Police Brutality, Corruption and Oppression in America.
N. Chesterfield, Va.: New Century Books, 2015.

Fox, Margalit. "Carolyn Bryant Donham Dies at 88; Her Words
Doomed Emmett Till." *The New York Times,* April 27, 2023.

Frank, Anne. *Anne Frank's Tales from the Secret Annex.*
New York: Washington Square Books / Pocket Books, 1983.

_____. *The Diary of a Young Girl.*
Introduction By Eleanor Roosevelt.
New York: Bantam Books, 1993. *Tim Cole, in* Selling the
Holocaust, *states that the Introduction by Eleanor Roosevelt*

*was actually written by Barbara Zimmerman, an editor at
Doubleday and only signed by Ms. Roosevelt.*

Frank, Otto and Miriam Pressler, eds.
Anne Frank: The Definitive Edition.
New York: Doubleday, 1995.
The edition that usually can be used for study of the Diary.

Gies, Miep. *Anne Frank Remembered:*
The Story of the Woman Who Helped Hide the Frank Family.
New York: Simon and Schuster, 1987.
*Written by the family friend who was the main contact
between those in the Secret Annex and the outside world.*

Gilbert, Martin. *The Holocaust:*
A History of the Jews of Europe During the Second World War
New York: Henry Holt, 1985.
At 828 pages, a must-read encyclopedia of the Holocaust.

Halberstam, David. *The Fifties.* New York: Fawcett Books, 1993.
*Contains a concise 10-page summary of the Till lynching and
subsequent trial in Mississippi.*

Hannah-Jones, Nikole, Caitlin Roper, Ilena Silverman and
Jake Silverstein.
The 1619 Project.
New York: One World / Random House, 2021.

Harris, James Henry. *The Forbidden Word:*
*The Symbol and Sign of Evil in American Literature,
History and Culture.*
Eugene, Oregon. Cascade Books, 2012.
The N word.

Kulka, Otto Dov. *Landscapes of the Metropolis of Death: reflections on memory and imagination.*
Cambridge: Belknap Press, 2013.
He was in Auschwitz as a child and in an children's choir and decades later remembered singing "Ode to Joy" within eyesight of a crematorium.

Langer, Emily. "Carolyn Bryant, elusive accuser in the lynching of Emmett Till, dies at 88." *The Washington Post*, April 27, 2023.

Levin, Meyer, 'The Dairy of a Young Girl."
The New York Times, June 15, 1952.
The first publication by Levin in the U.S. about the diary; Levin began a life-long obsession that he should be the only person to edit, publish and / or comment on the diary. This lead to a decades-long feud with Anne Frank's father. Levin carried this obsession to his grave.

Levy, Primo. *If This is a Man.*
London: Orion Press, 1947.

Lindwer, Willy. *The Last Seven Months of Anne Frank.*
New York: Pantheon Books, 1991.
Based on a previous documentary film of the same name.

Luscombe, Richard. "Virginia governor blocks bill banning police from seeking menstrual records."
The Guardian, Feb. 16, 2023.

McCarthy, Cormac. *The Road.*
New York: Knopf, 2006.

Müller, Melissa *Anne Frank: The Biography.*
New York: Henry Holt Co., 1998.

Nordan, Lewis. *Wolf Whistle.* Chapel Hill: Algonquin Books, 1993.
    *A fictionalized account of the Till case and the South during
    those years.*

Parks, Rosa. *Rosa Parks: My Story. New York:* Dial Books, 1992.
    Memoir of her life; no mention of Emmett Till.

Prose, Francine. *Anne Frank: The book, the life, the afterlife.*
    New York: HarperCollins, 2009.

Serwer, Adam. "Why don't we remember Ike as a civil rights
leader?" MSNBC website, posted May 16, 2014.

Shirer, William L. *The Rise and Fall of the Third Reich.*
    New York: Simon and Schuster, 1960.
    For decades, this has been the ultimate guide to Hitler's Reich.

Siegel, Nina. *The Diary Keepers: World War Two in the
Netherlands As Written by the People Who Lived Through It.*
    New York: The Ecco Press / Harper Collins, 2023.
    *At 471 pages, plus supplemental material, this has less than
    two pages about Anne Frank and her Diary.*

Spiegelman, Art. *Maus.* New York,. Pantheon, 1973
    The Holocaust as a graphic novel. Highly acclaimed.

Springle, Ray. *In the Land of Jim Crow.*
    New York: Simon and Schuster, 1949.
    *This expedition by a white man into the segregated South pre-
    dates Griffin's Black Like Me.*

Steinbeck, John. *The Grapes of Wrath.*
    New York: The Viking Press, 1939.
    Widely known as the premier novel of The Great Depression.

Till. DVD. Orion Pictures, 2023.

Till-Mobley, Mamie and Christopher Benson. *Death of Innocence: The Story of the Hate Crime That Changed America.* New York: One World / Random House, 2003.

Tyson, Timothy B. *The Blood of Emmett Till.* New York: Simon and Schuster, 2017.

The Untold Story of Emmett Louis Till. DVD. ThinkFilm Co., 2005.

Whitfield, Stephen J. *A Death in the Delta: The Story of Emmett Till.* Baltimore: Johns Hopkins University Press, 1988.

Wilkerson, Isabel. *Caste: The Origins of Our Discontents.* New York: Random House, 2020.
She postulates that the origins of the Nuremberg Laws in Nazi Germany may well have been the Jim Crow laws, established decades earlier in the United States.

______. *The Warmth of Other Suns: The Epic Story of America's Great Migration.* New York: Knopf, 2011.
How Southern Blacks and others permanently moved in record numbers from the rural south into the urban North.

Yang, Maya. "Emmett Till relative's lawsuit seeks to serve white woman's arrest warrant." The Guardian. Feb. 11, 2023.
How a southern sheriff had a valid arrest warrant for Carolyn Bryant in 1955, but didn't serve it because he "didn't want to disturb her."

Websites

www.annefrank.org

www.annefrank.com

https://tillapt.emmett-till.org

https: //emmetttilllegacyfoundation. com

Index

Sources

Page

10   "But in the turmoil of defeat…" Martin Gilbert, *The Holocaust*, pp. 23.

34   "She was a marvelous …" and "The ardor in her..,." in Philip Roth, *The Ghost Writer*, pp. 169-170.

38   "Mr. Frank was…" in Miep Gies, *Anne Frank Remembered*, 122.

41   "Once Miep closed…" in Melissa Müller, *Anne Frank: The Biography*, pp. 164-165.

46-47   "My entire hope lies with…" Otto. Frank, letter to his Mother May 15, 1945.

48-49   "frozen little birds…" "He read slowly…" Karen Bartlett, *The Diary That Changed the World*, pp. 42, 43.

49   "I read on and on…" Otto Frank letter to his mother.

54   "26 different techniques…" in Thomas Fensch, *Writing Solutions: Beginnings, Middles and Endings.* (2001). pp. 23-151.

54   "Anne Frank's diary …" Meyer Levin, *New York Times Book Review*, June 15, 1952.

56   "Invariably, the first book …" Bartlett, pp. 80.

72   "He woke in the night…" Cormac McCarthy, *The Road*, pp. 87.

76   "Since the 1950s …" Tim Cole, *Selling the Holocaust*, pp. 23.

97   "Hitler had studied…" Isabel Wilkerson, *Caste: The Origins of Our Discontents*, pp. 81.

101   "Two cents worth ... " and "Till was murdered ..."
        In Stephen J. Whitfield, *A Death in the Delta*, pp. 144
        and 141, respectively.

102   "They left as if under a spell ..." Isabel Wilkerson,
        The Warmth of Other Suns, pp. 8-9.

103   "We had come to Argo ..." and "little Mississippi ..."
        Mamie Till-Mobley, *Death of Innocence*, pp. 19 and 18,
        respectively.

104   "Somewhere around seven ..." *Death of Innocence*,
        pp. 121.

109   "J.J. Breland ..." Timothy Tyson, *The Blood of Emmett
        Till*, pp. 49.

114   " ... a 270-pound former football player ... "
        in Tyson, pp. 46. "... the Miland and Bryants ..."
        Tyson.

116   "By the time ..." Whitfield, *A Death in the Delta*,
        pp. 37-38.

120   "Well, what else ..." Huie, *Look* magazine.

121   "The shock of ..." Whitfield, pp.71.

122   "In two terms as president ..." Serwer column.

128   "Nothing that boy did ..." in Tyson pp. 7.

130   "He was a hell of a fine fellow ..." in Whitfield
        pp. 144.

About the Author

THOMAS FENSCH began publishing books in 1970; this is now his 45th book of nonfiction.

His 1979 book, *Steinbeck and Covici: The Story of a Friendship* was the first analysis of the decades-long relationship between John Steinbeck and his editor-publisher Pascal Covici. It was highly reviewed in *The New York Times* and widely reviewed elsewhere and has long been considered a seminal work in Steinbeck scholarship. It has been continuously in print since 1979. He has also published four other books on Steinbeck and has lectured about Steinbeck in the United States and Japan.

He is also the principal biographer of John Howard Griffin, who dyed his skin black and toured the South in the pre-Civil Rights days of the late 1950s. Griffin subsequently published *Black Like Me*, which became—and still is—an American classic.

Fensch's biography *The Man Who Changed His Skin: The Life and Work of John Howard Griffin* was published in 2011.

Fensch has a doctorate from Syracuse University in print communication and live outside Richmond, Va, with a posse of dogs, his Senior Literary Advisors, who are always ready to fetch yellow pencils, legal pads and the like.